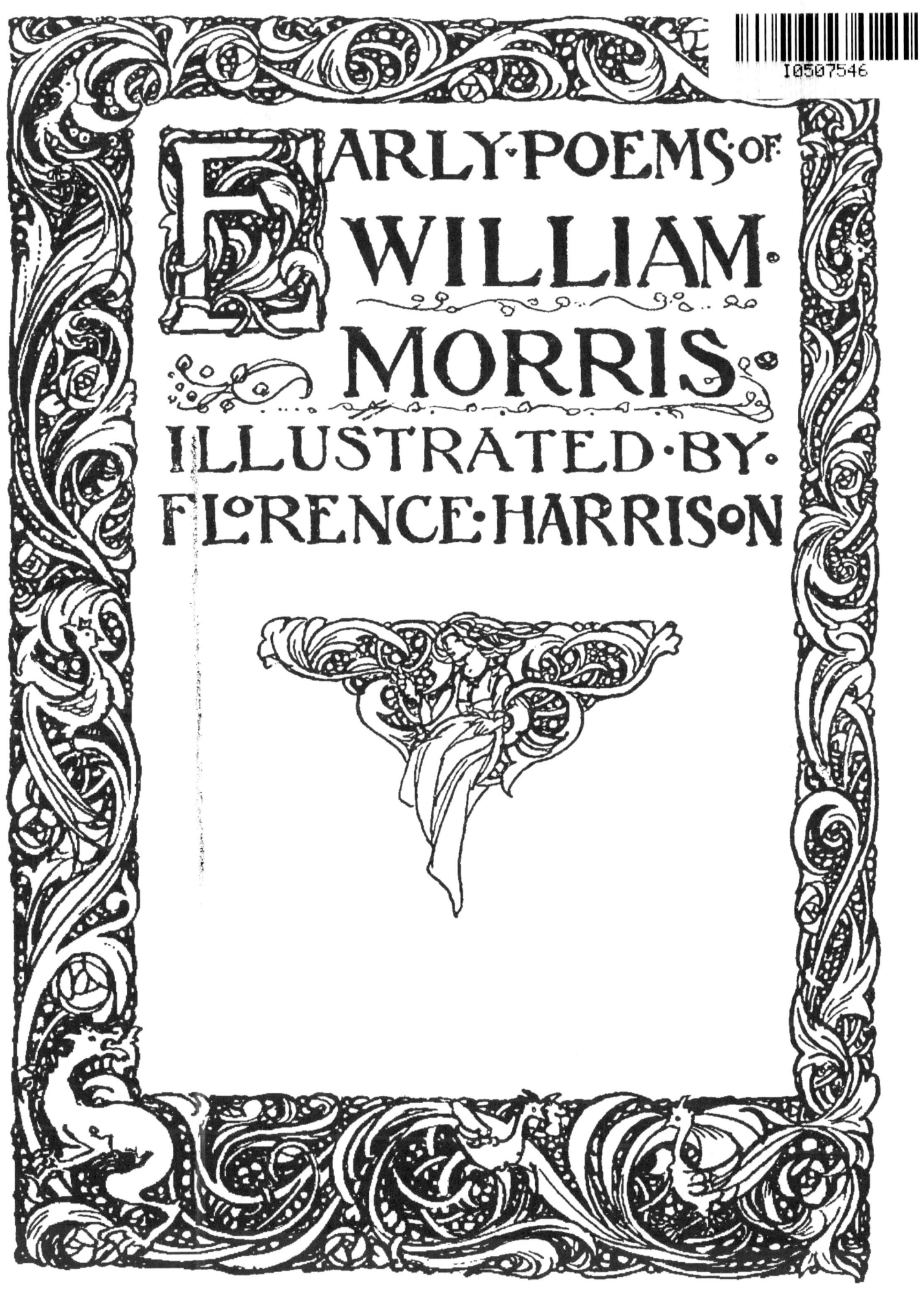

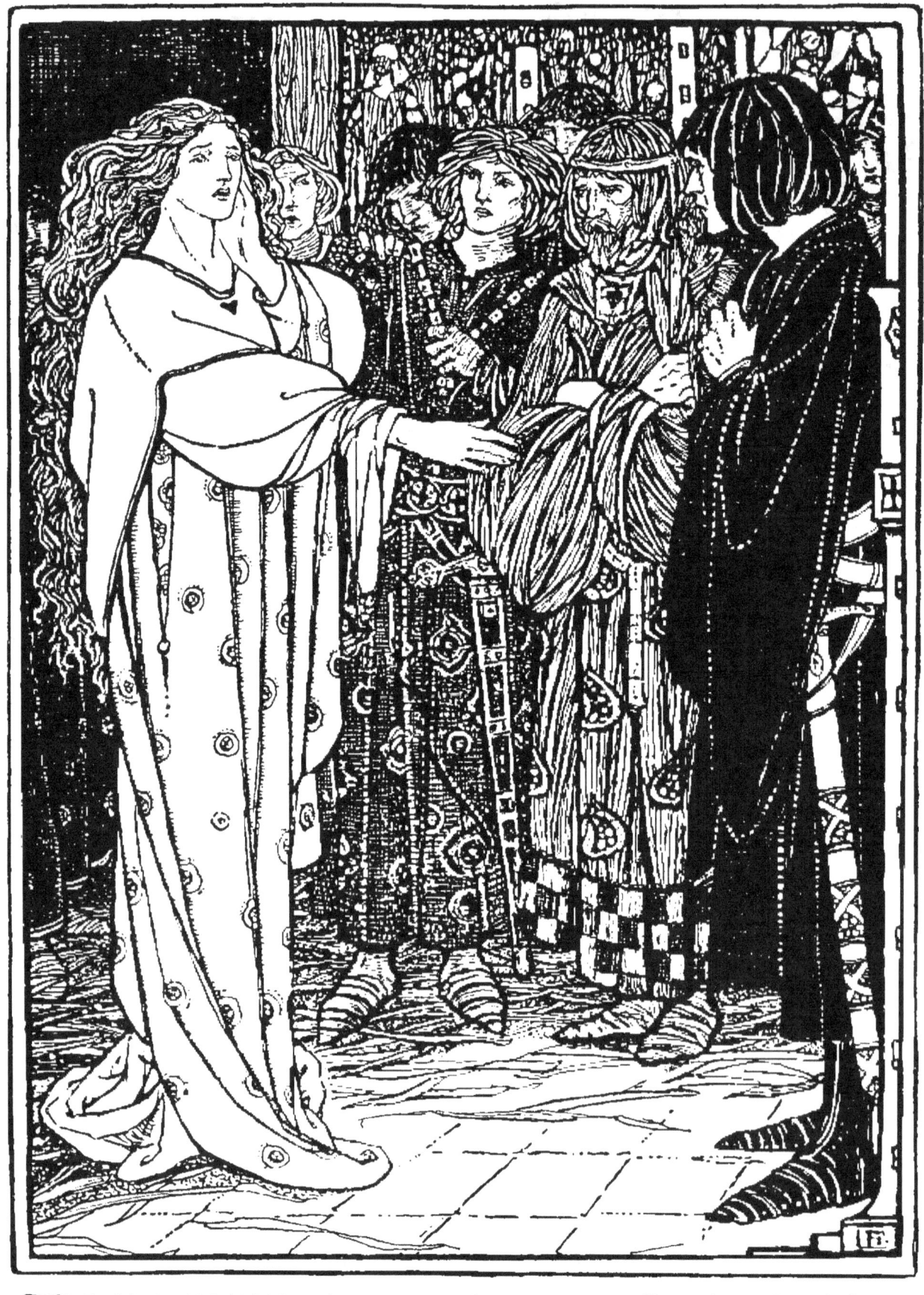

NEVERTHELESS·YOU·O·SIR·GAUWAINE·LIE·

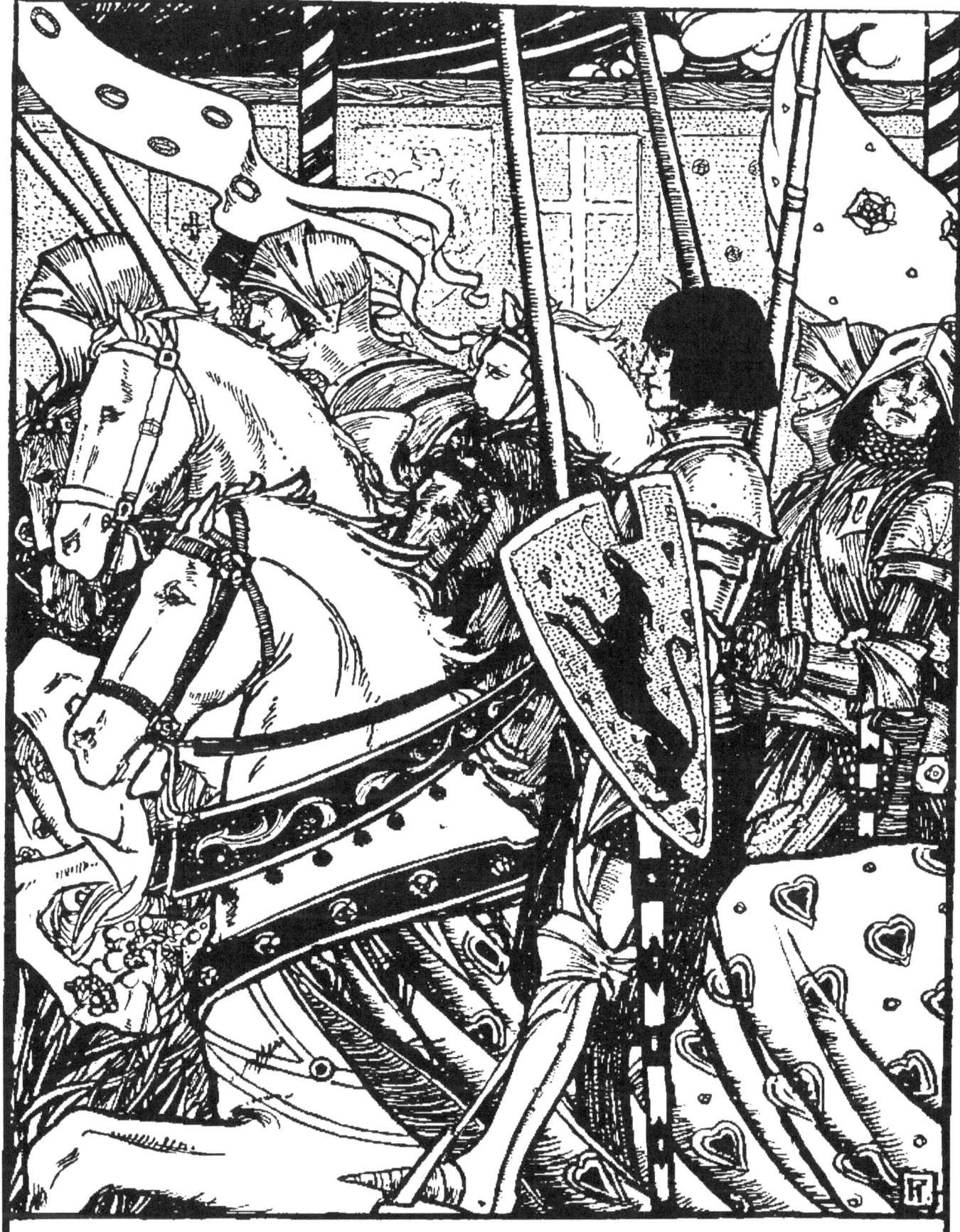

AND BY HIM PALOMYDES HELMET OFF HE FOUGHT

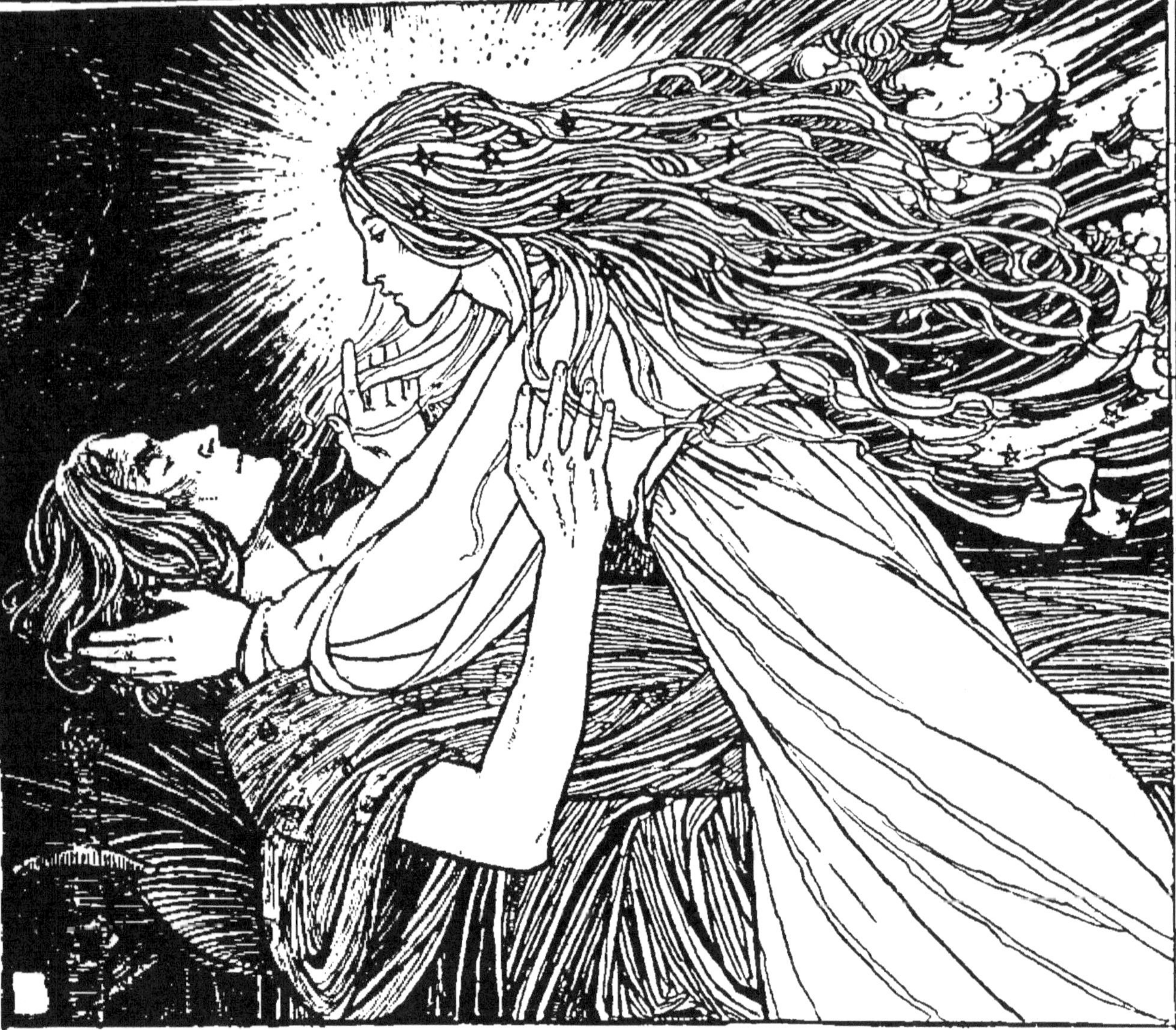

NO LONG TIME HENCE ALSO,
I SEE
THY WASTED FINGERS TWINE
WITHIN THE TRESSES OF HER
HAIR
THAT SHINETH GLORIOUSLY.

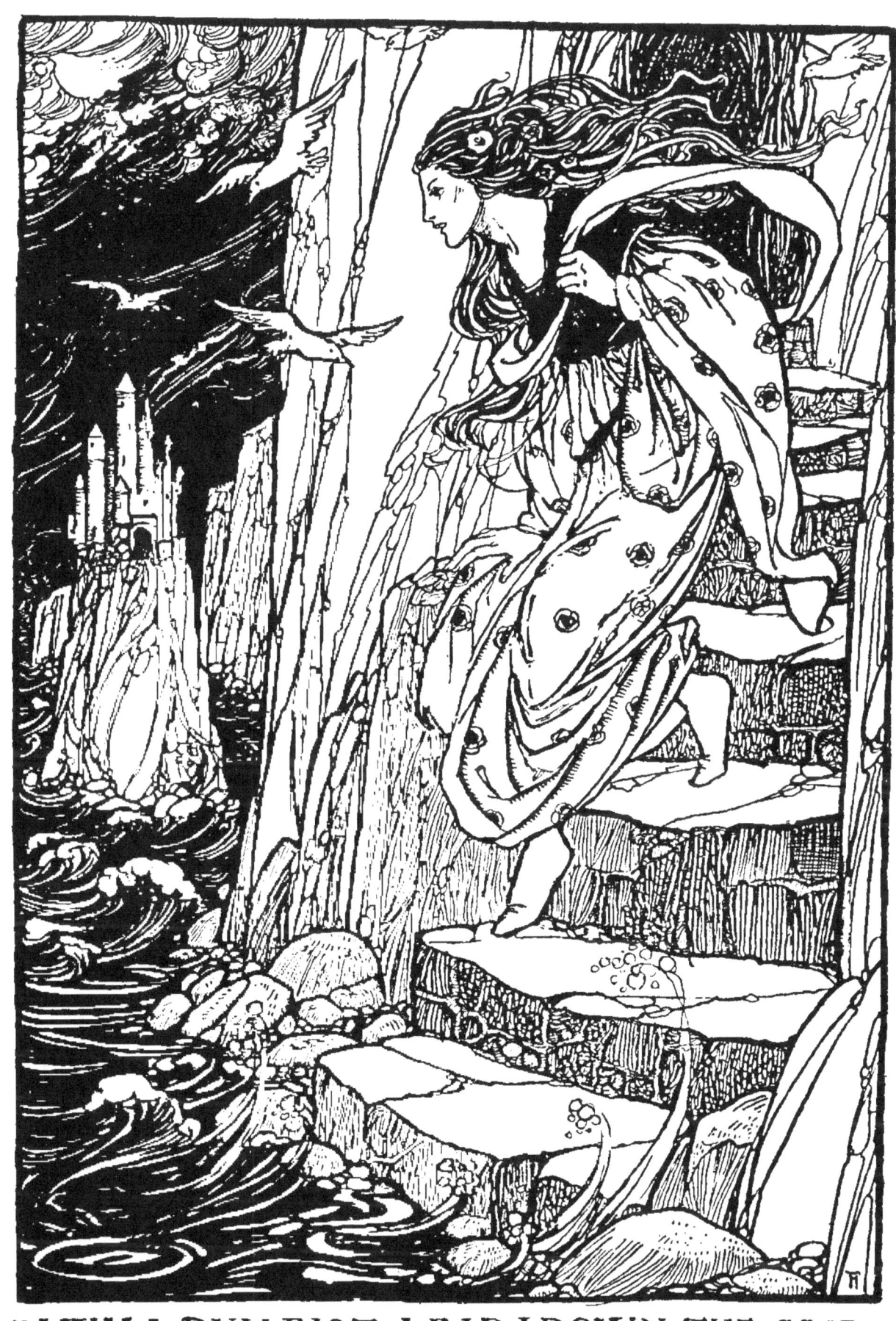

I WILL RUN FAST LEAP ADOWN THE SLIPPERY SEA STAIRS WHERE THE CRABS FIGHT

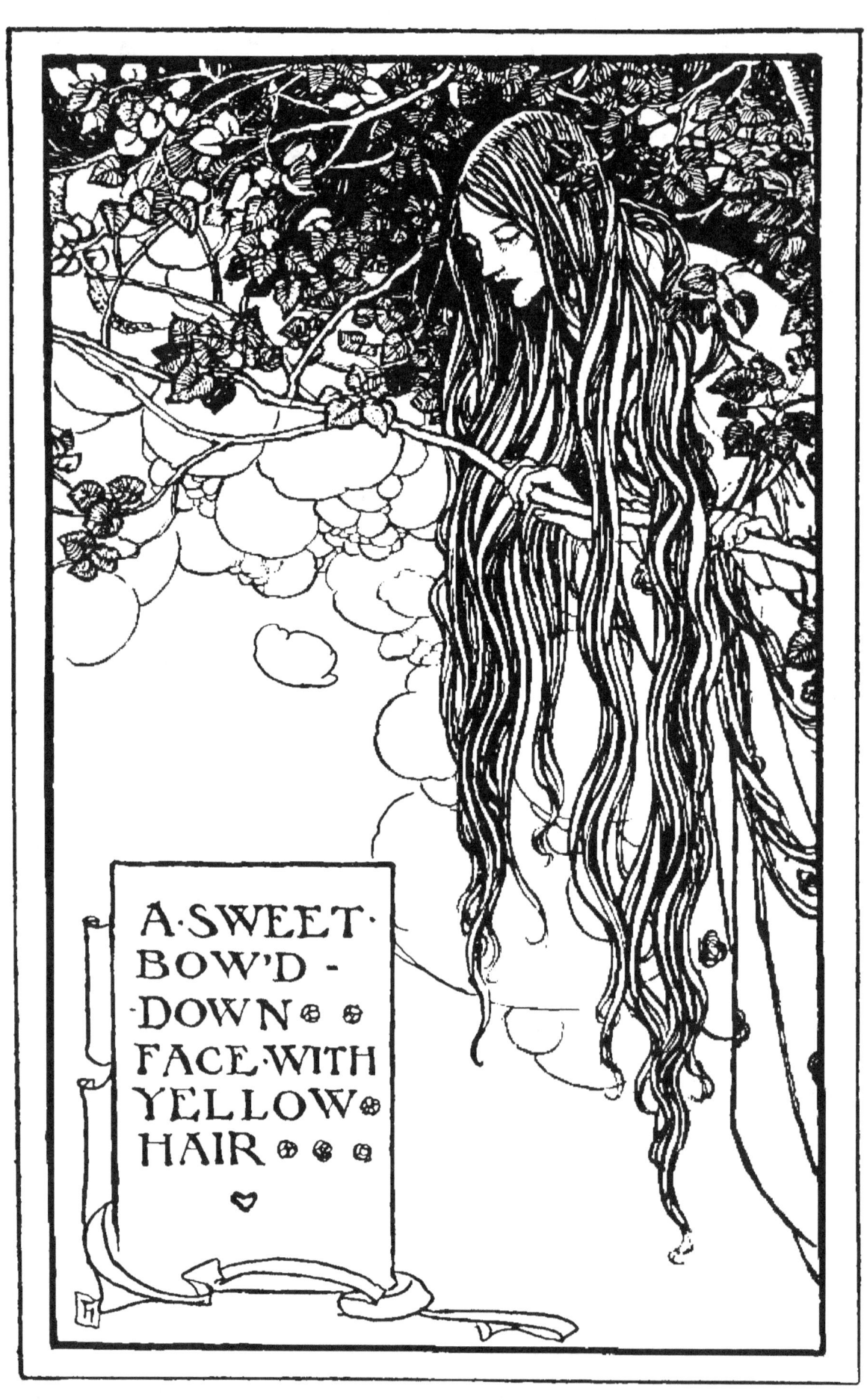

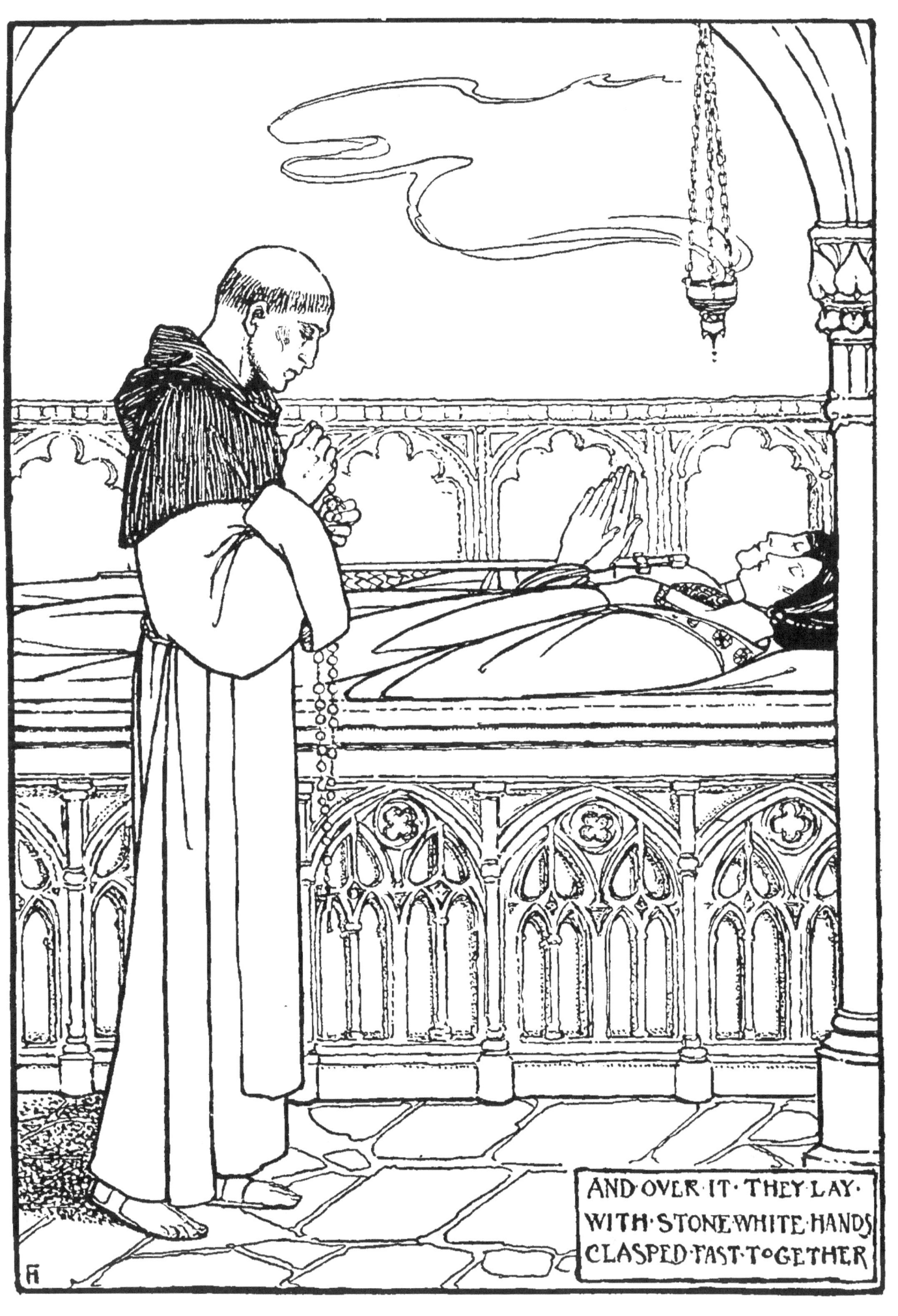

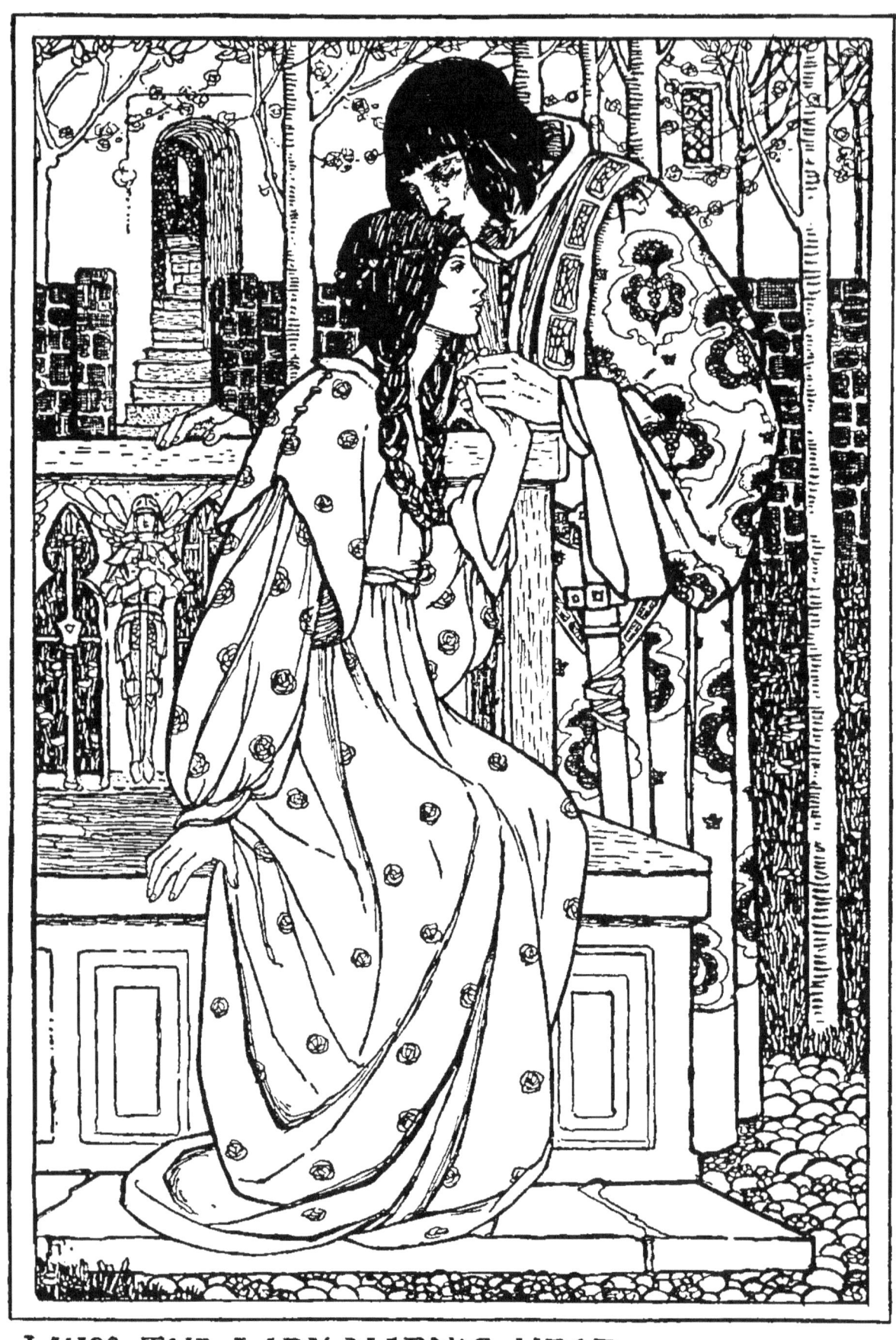

I KISS THE LADY MARY'S HEAD·
HER·LIPS·AND·HER·HAIR·GOLDEN·RED·
BECAUSE·TO·DAY·WE·HAVE·BEEN·WED·

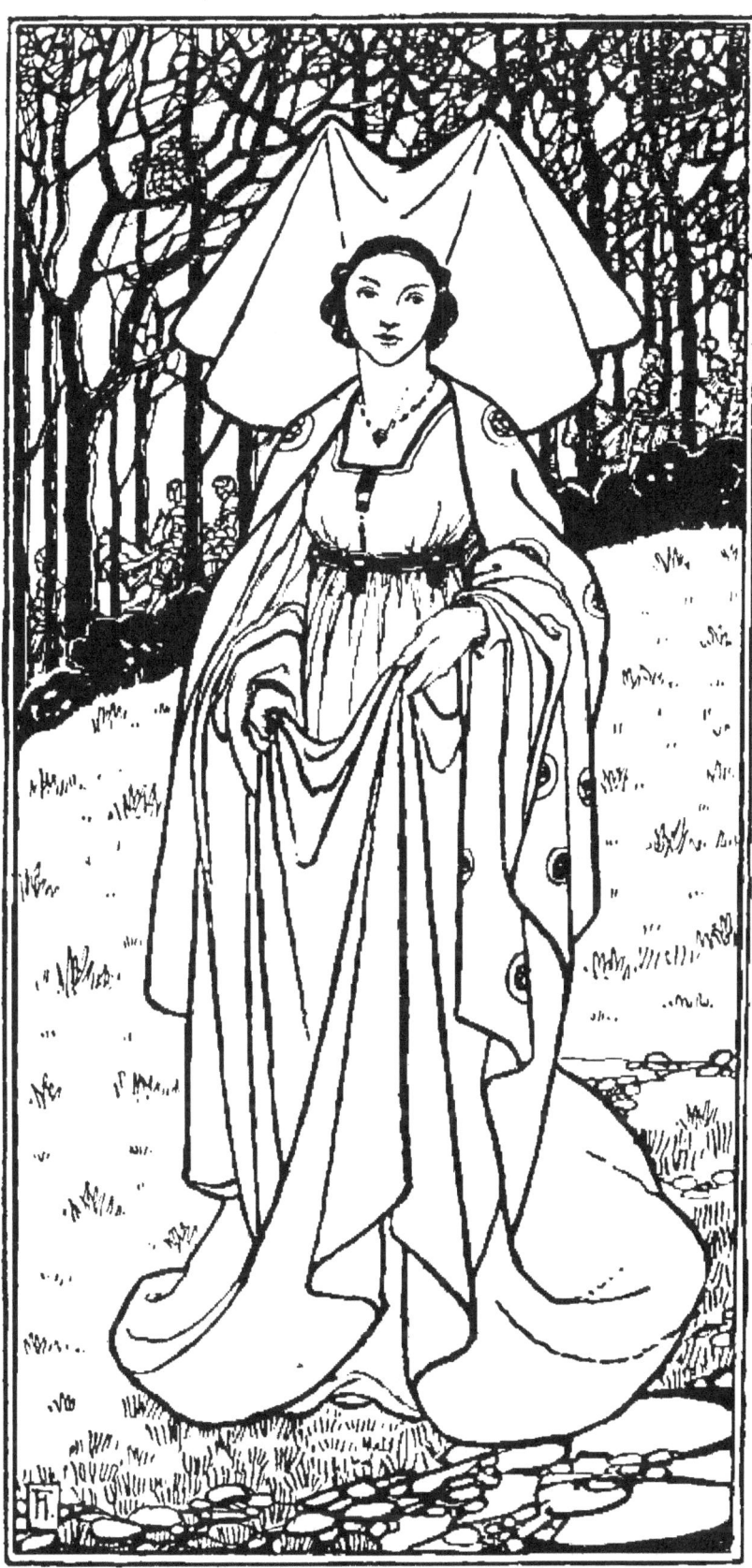

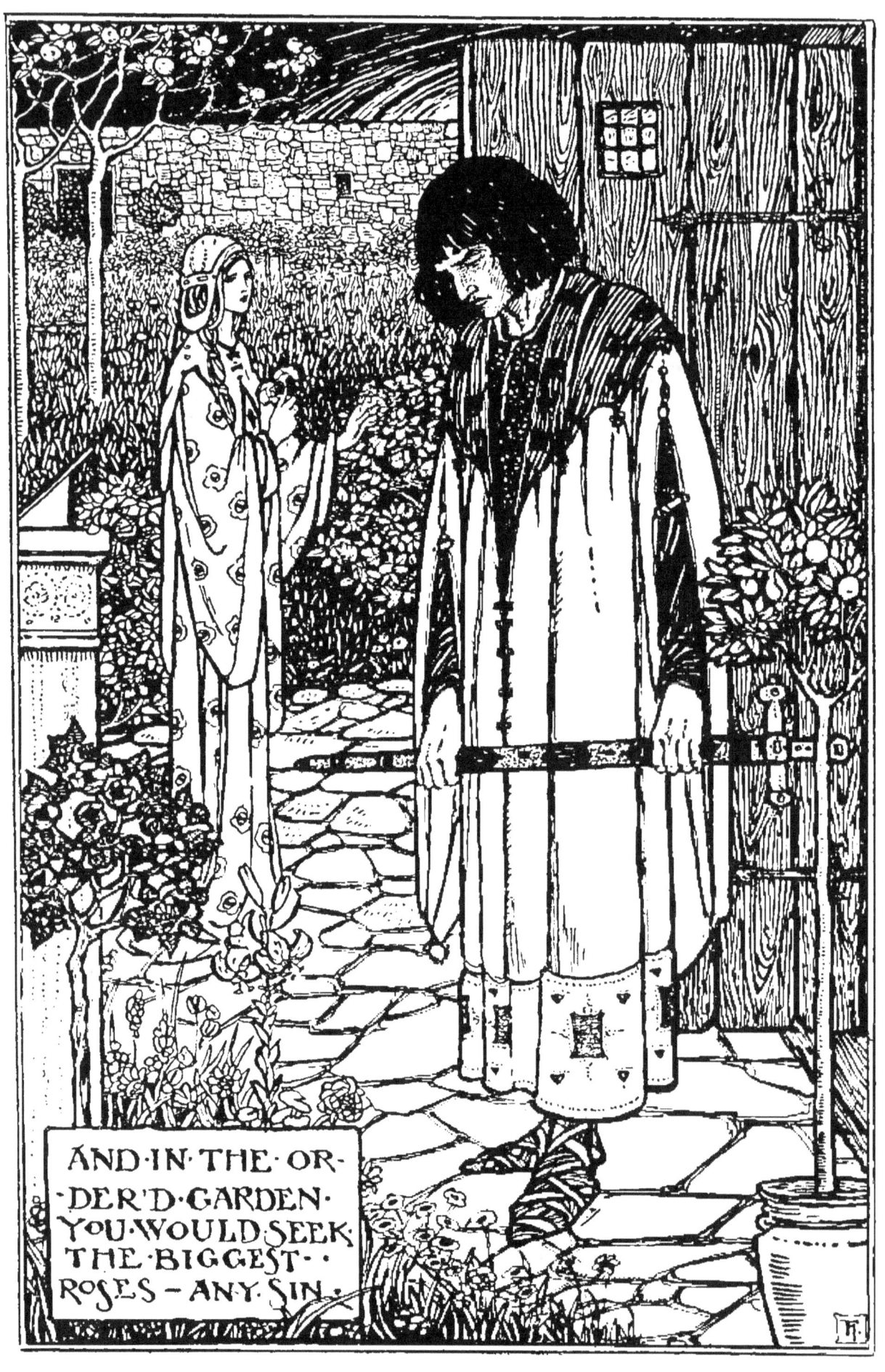

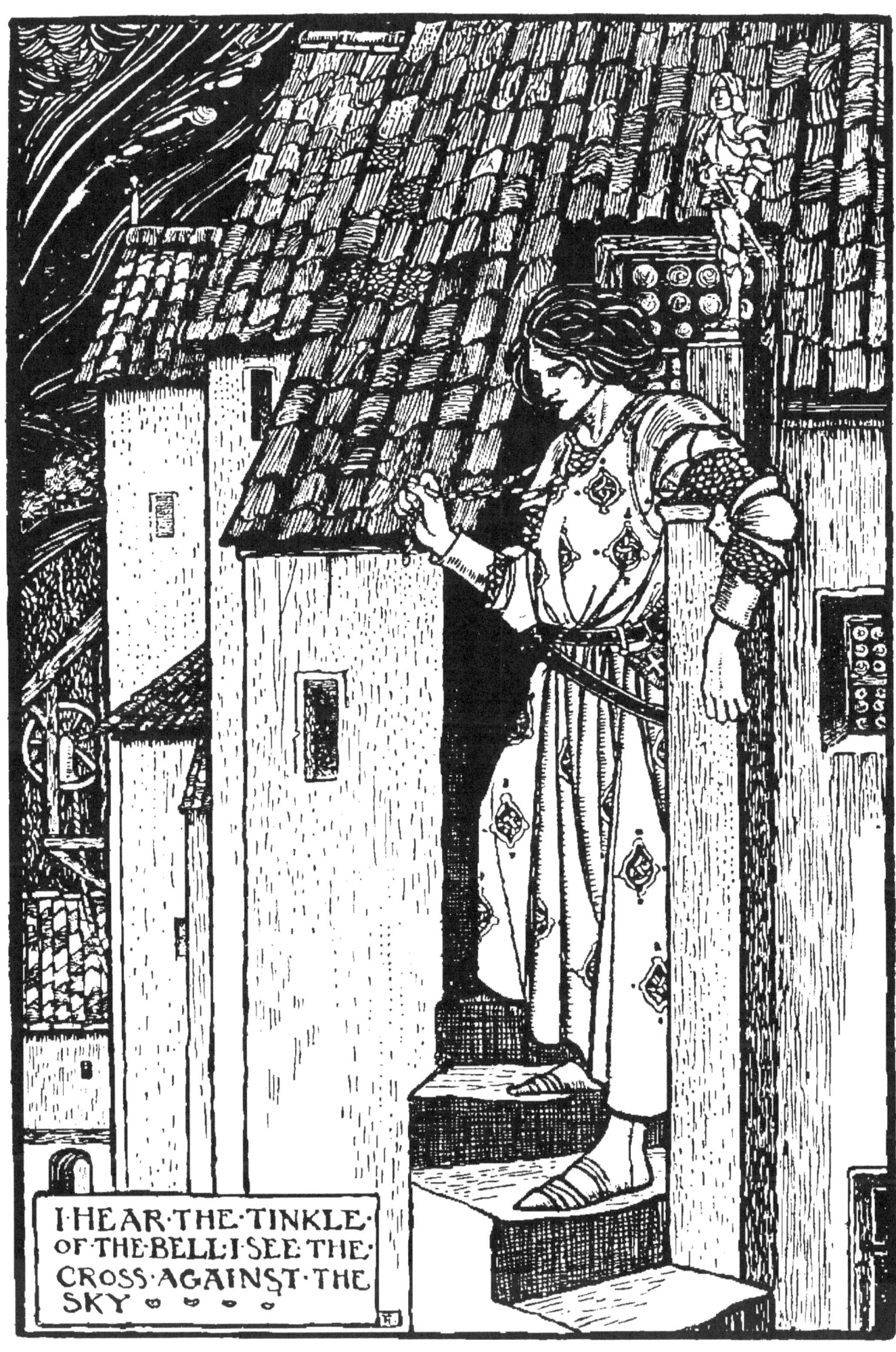

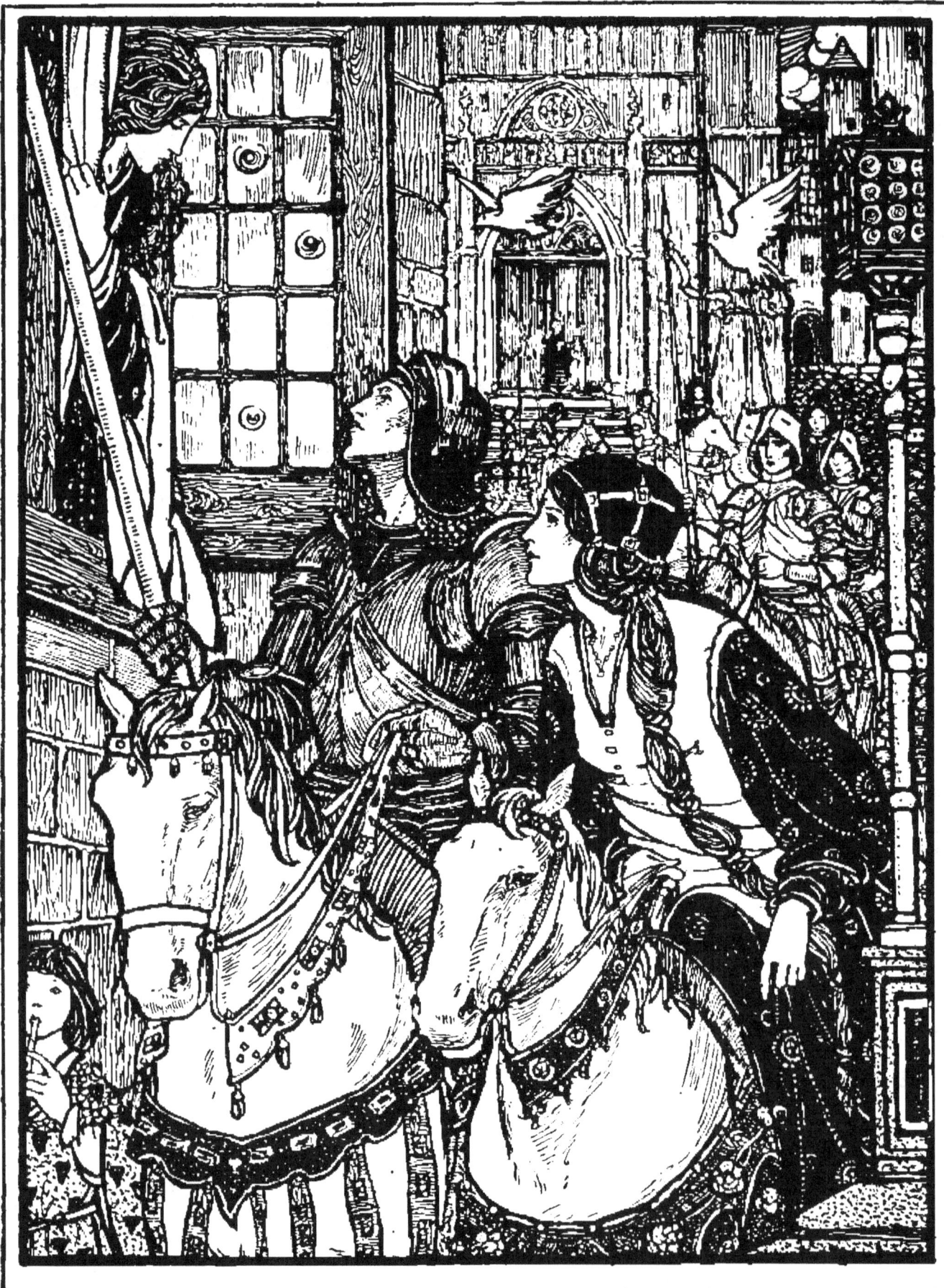

OH·WHY·DOES·YON·PALE·FACE·LOOK·AT·ME·
FROM·OUT·THE·GOLDEN·CLOTH·

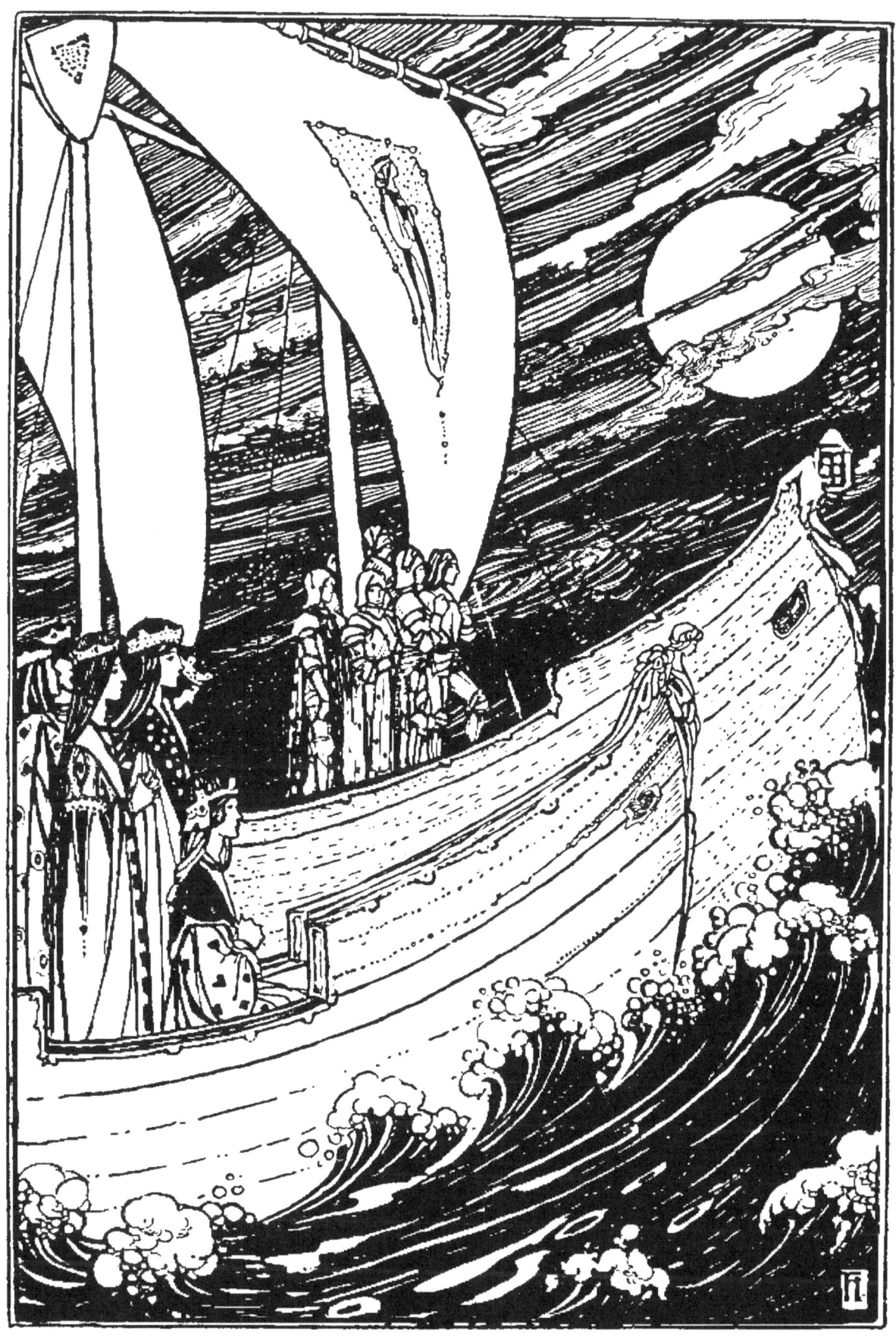

SIX MAIDENS ROUND THE MAST — A RED GOLD CROWN ON EVERY ONE · A GREEN GOWN ON THE LAST

Poems by Christina Rossetti

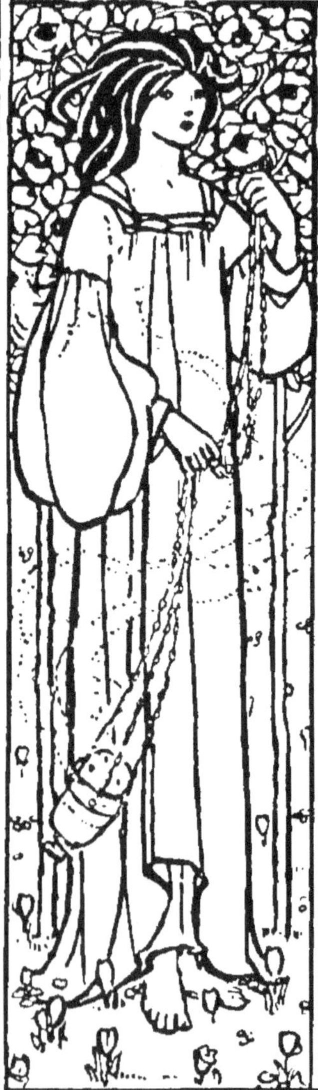

Illustrations by Florence Harrison

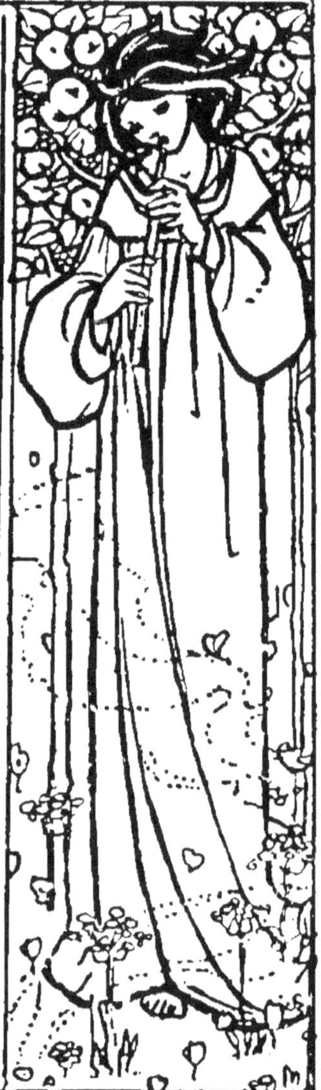

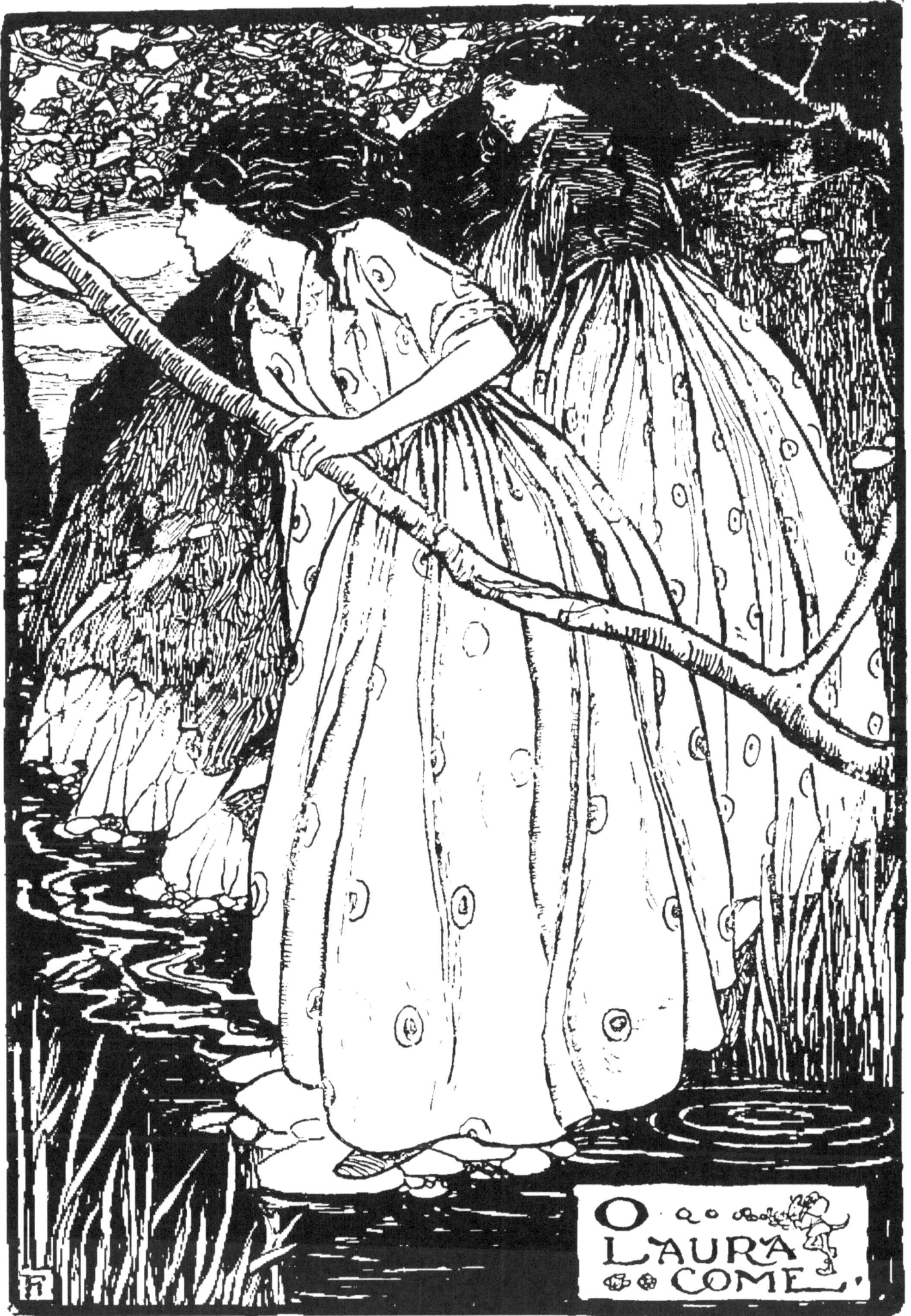

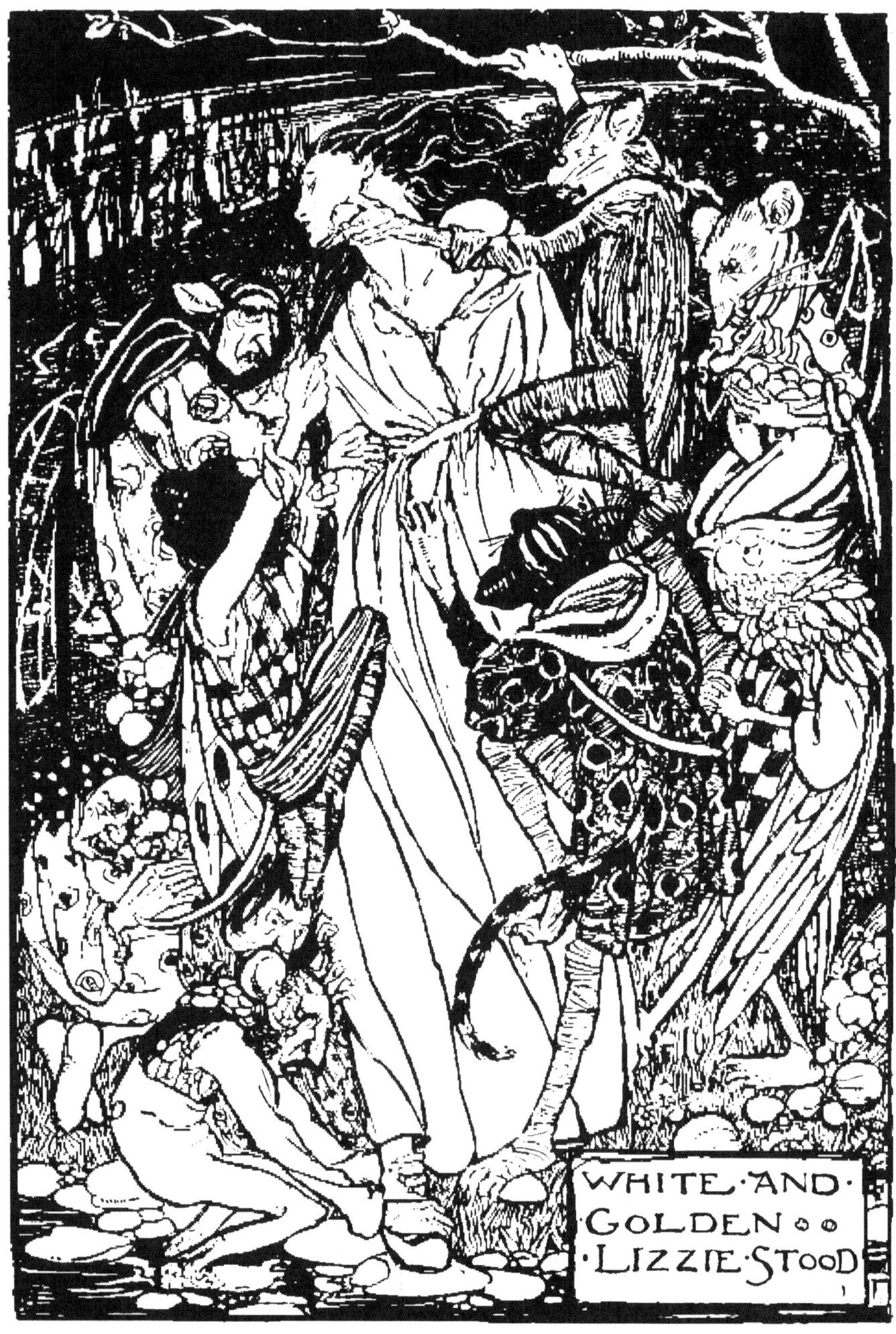

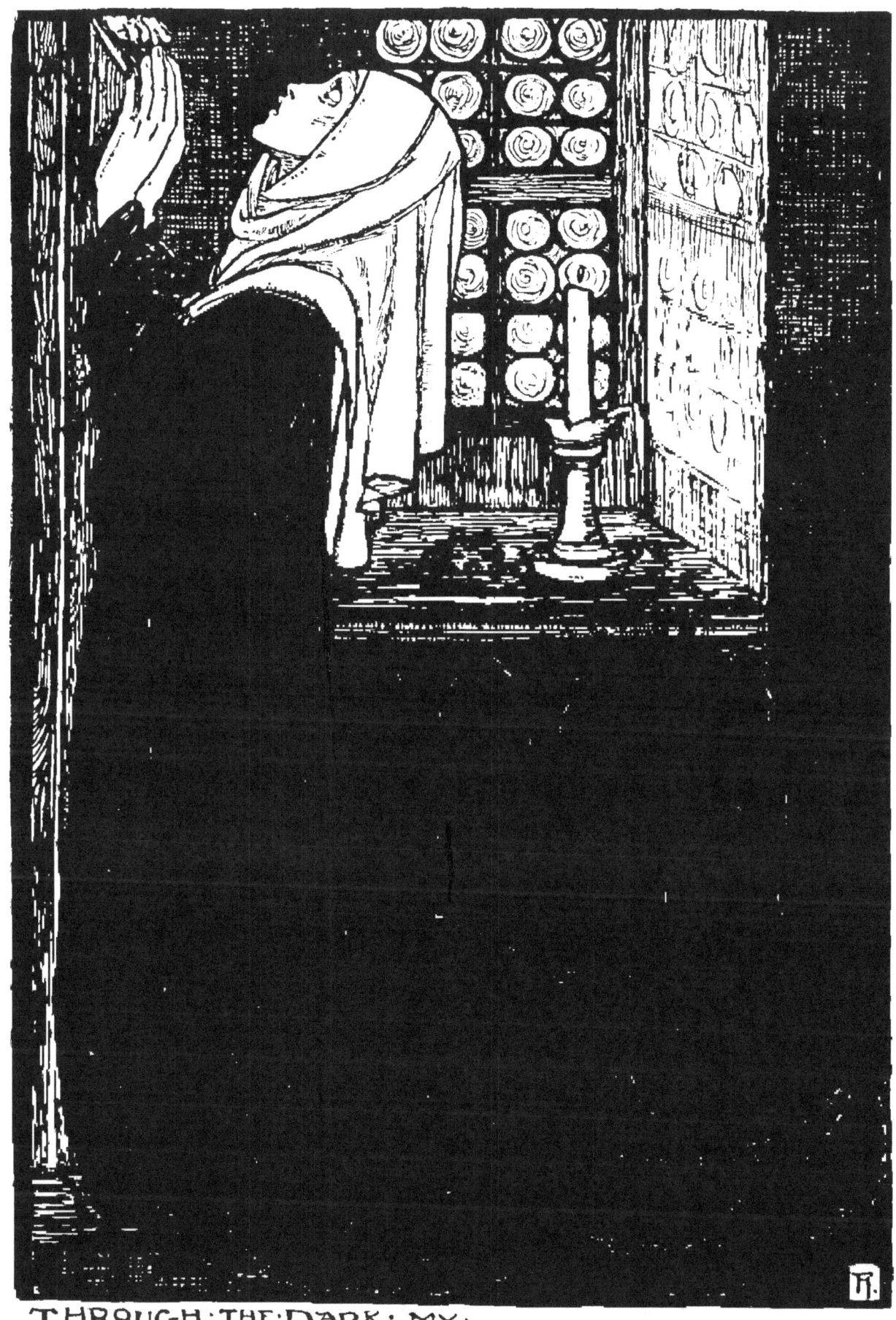

THROUGH THE DARK MY SILENCE SPOKE LIKE THUNDER.

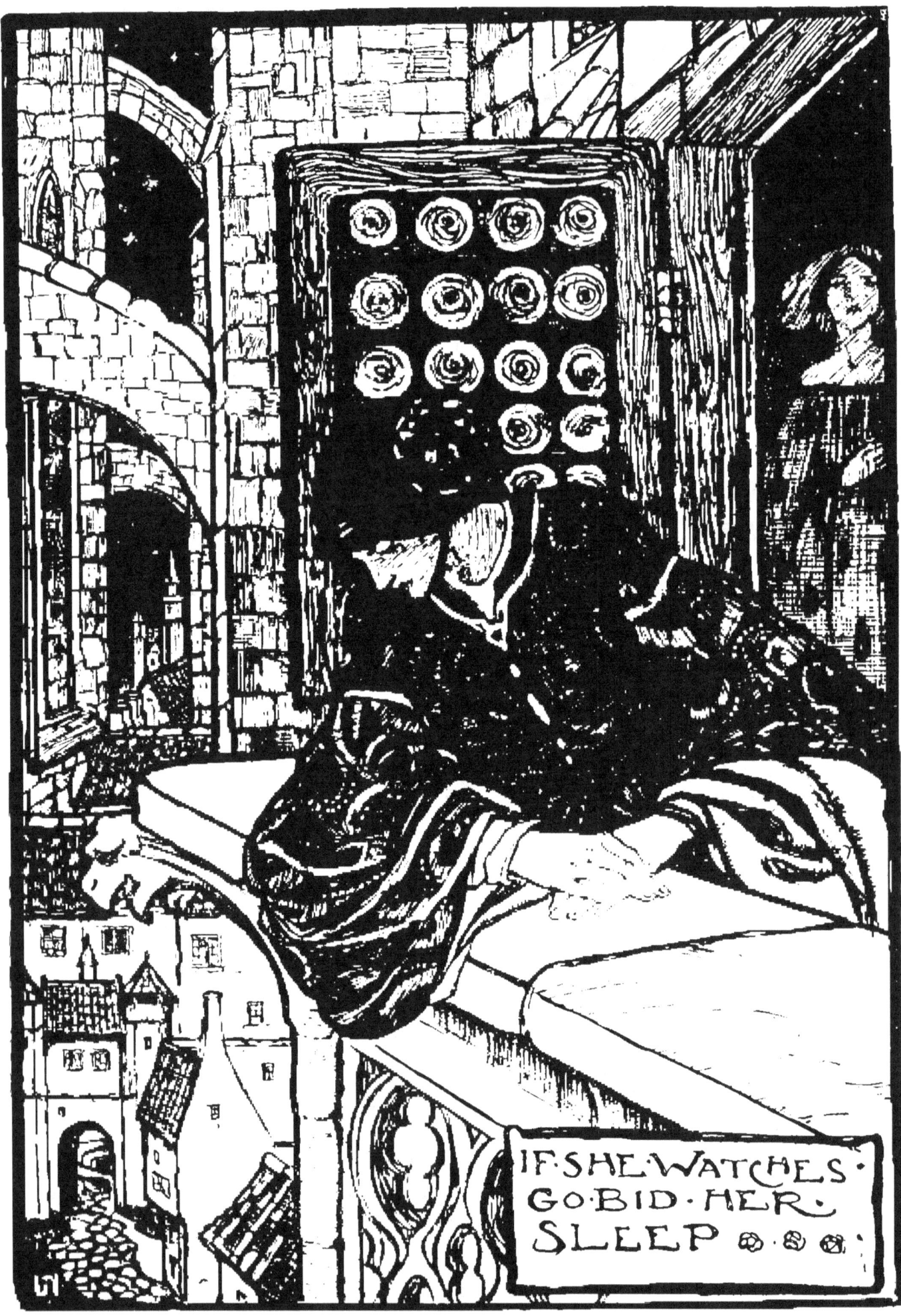

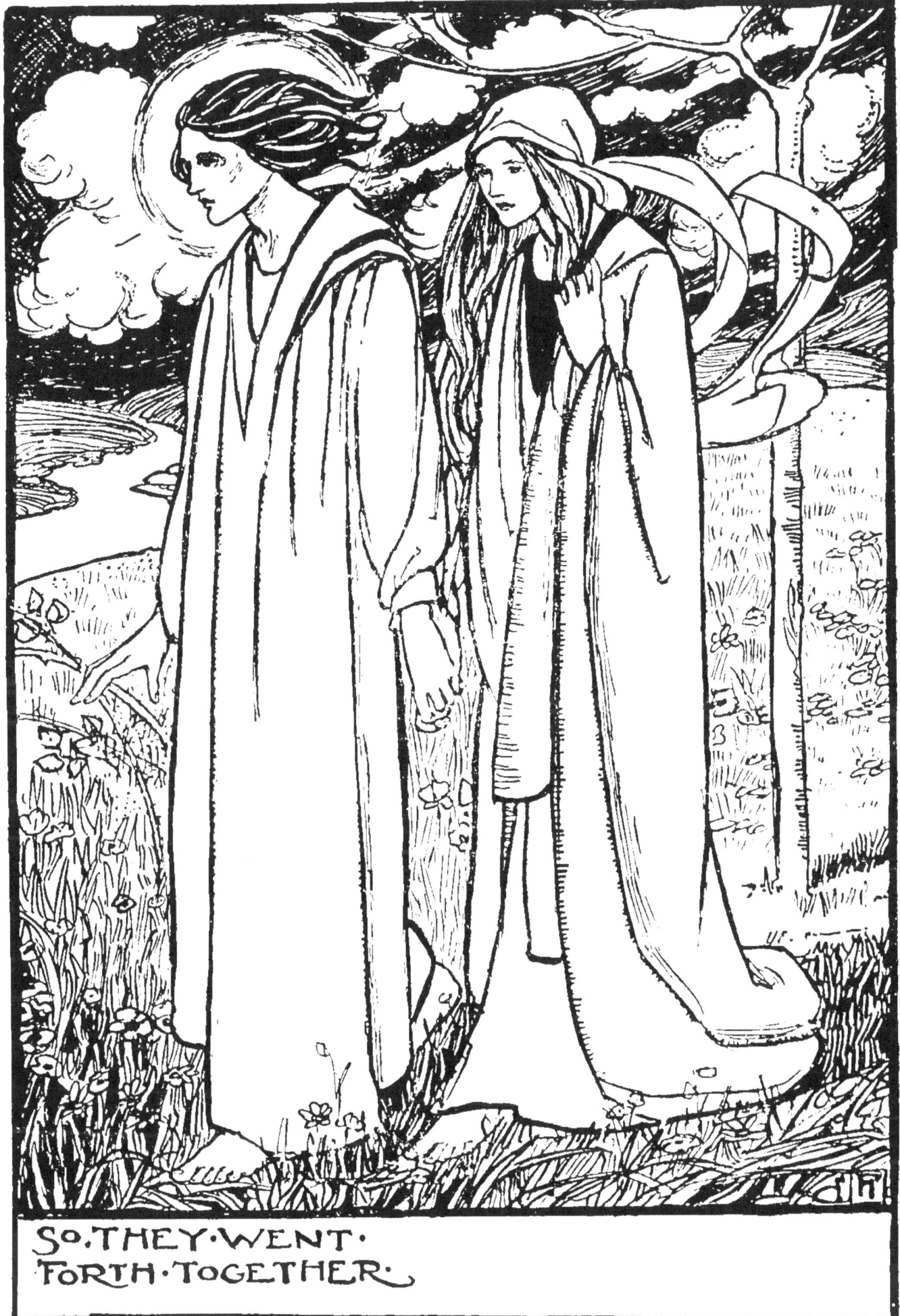

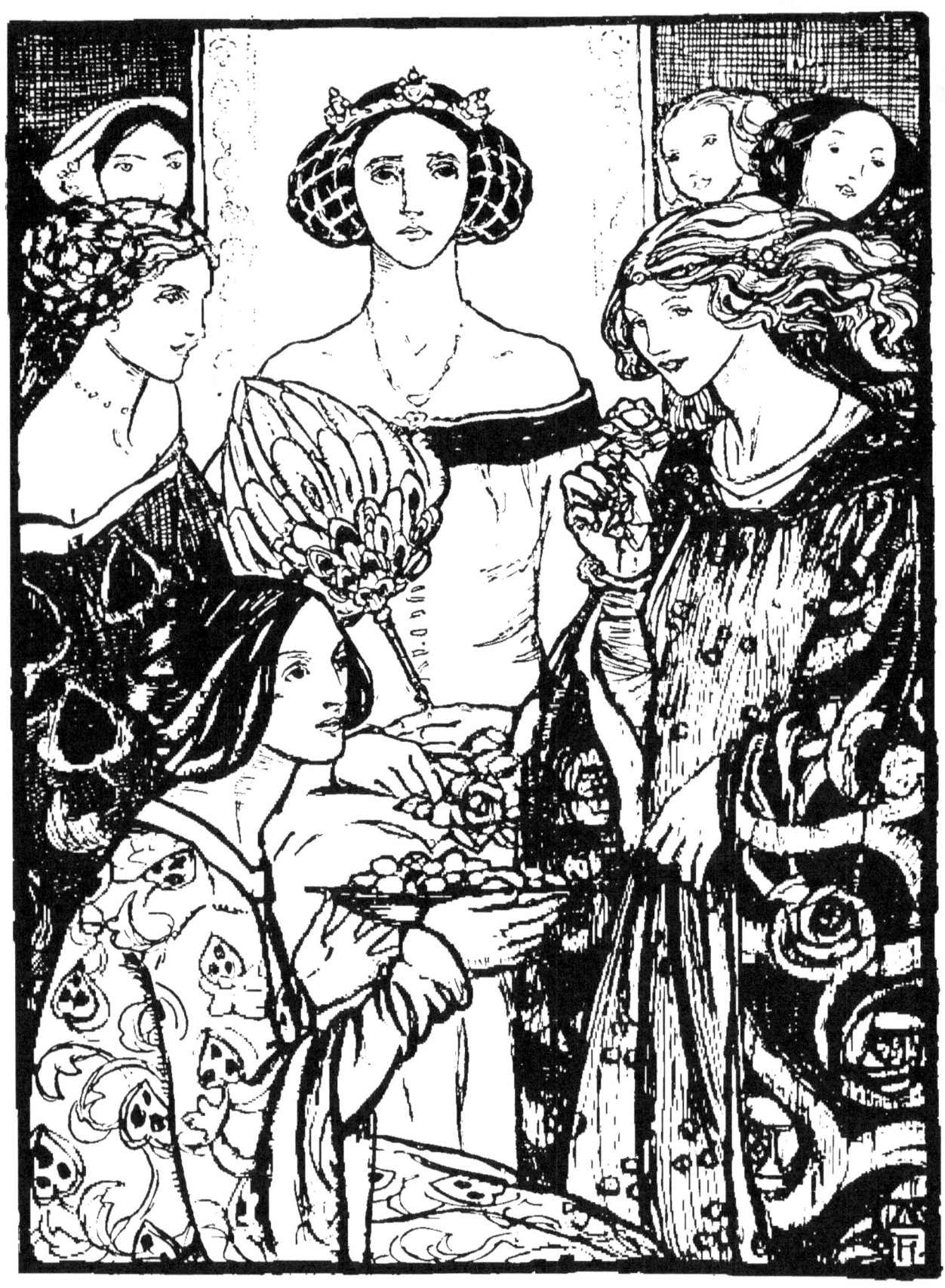

MY·LADIES·ALL·
ARE·FAIR·TO
GAZE·UPON·

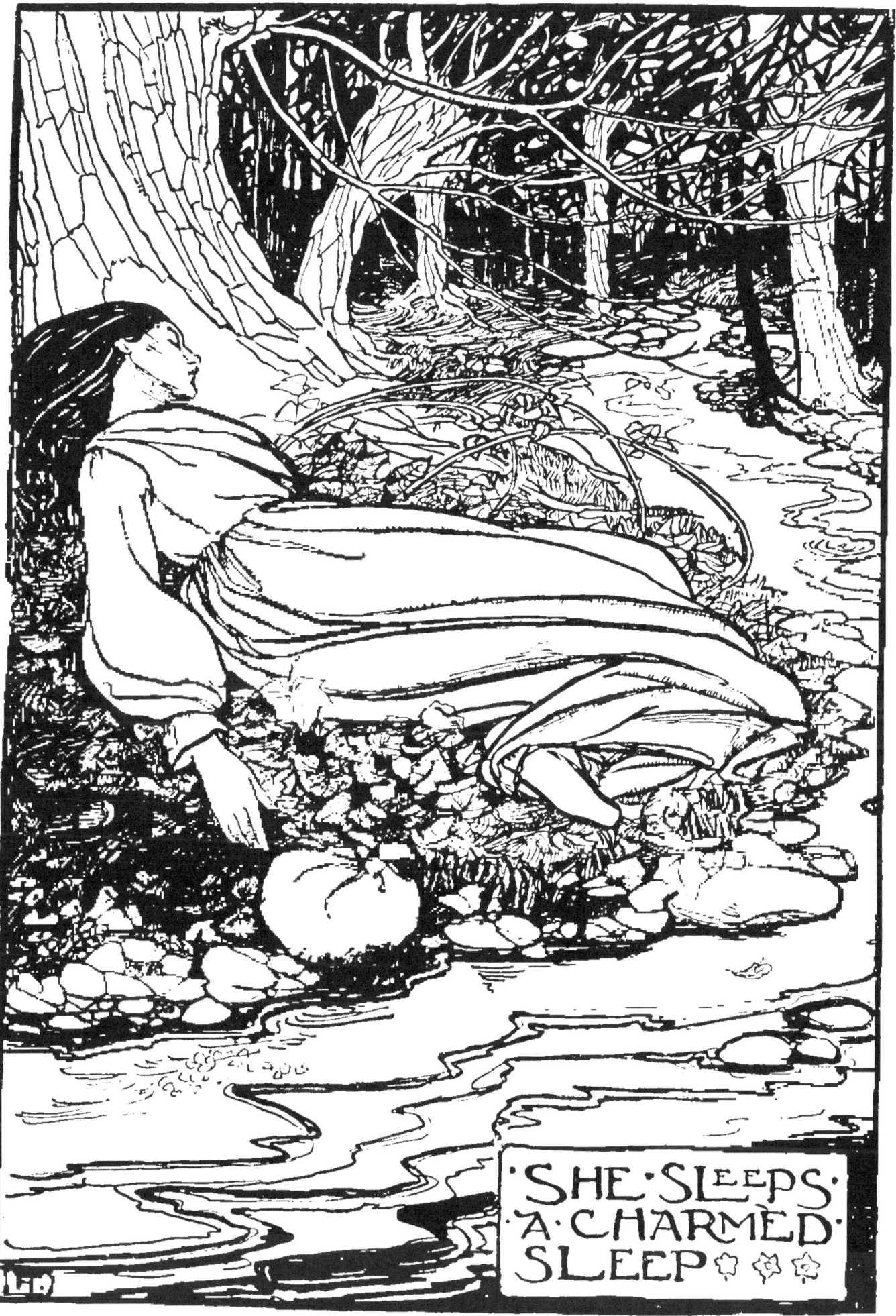

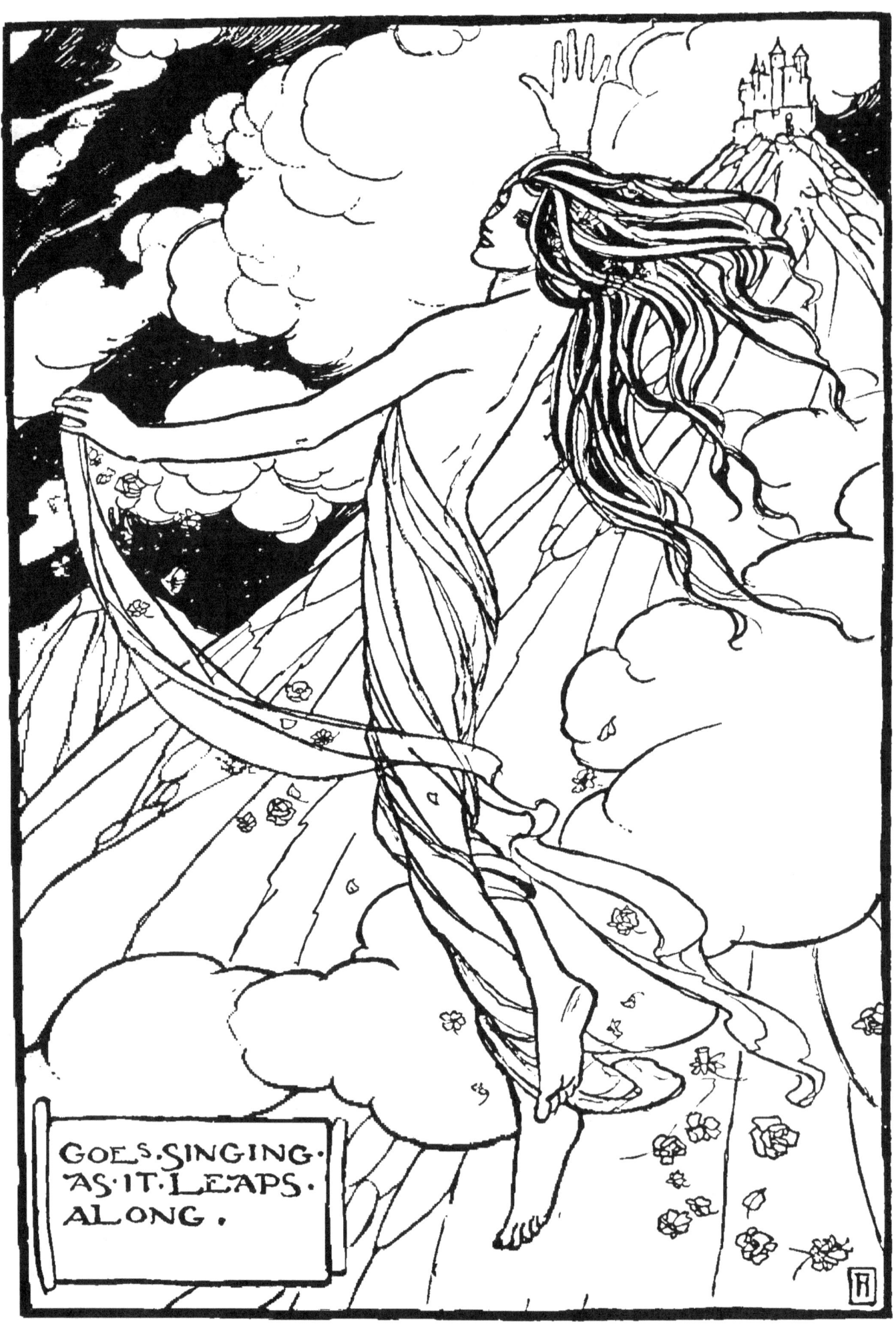

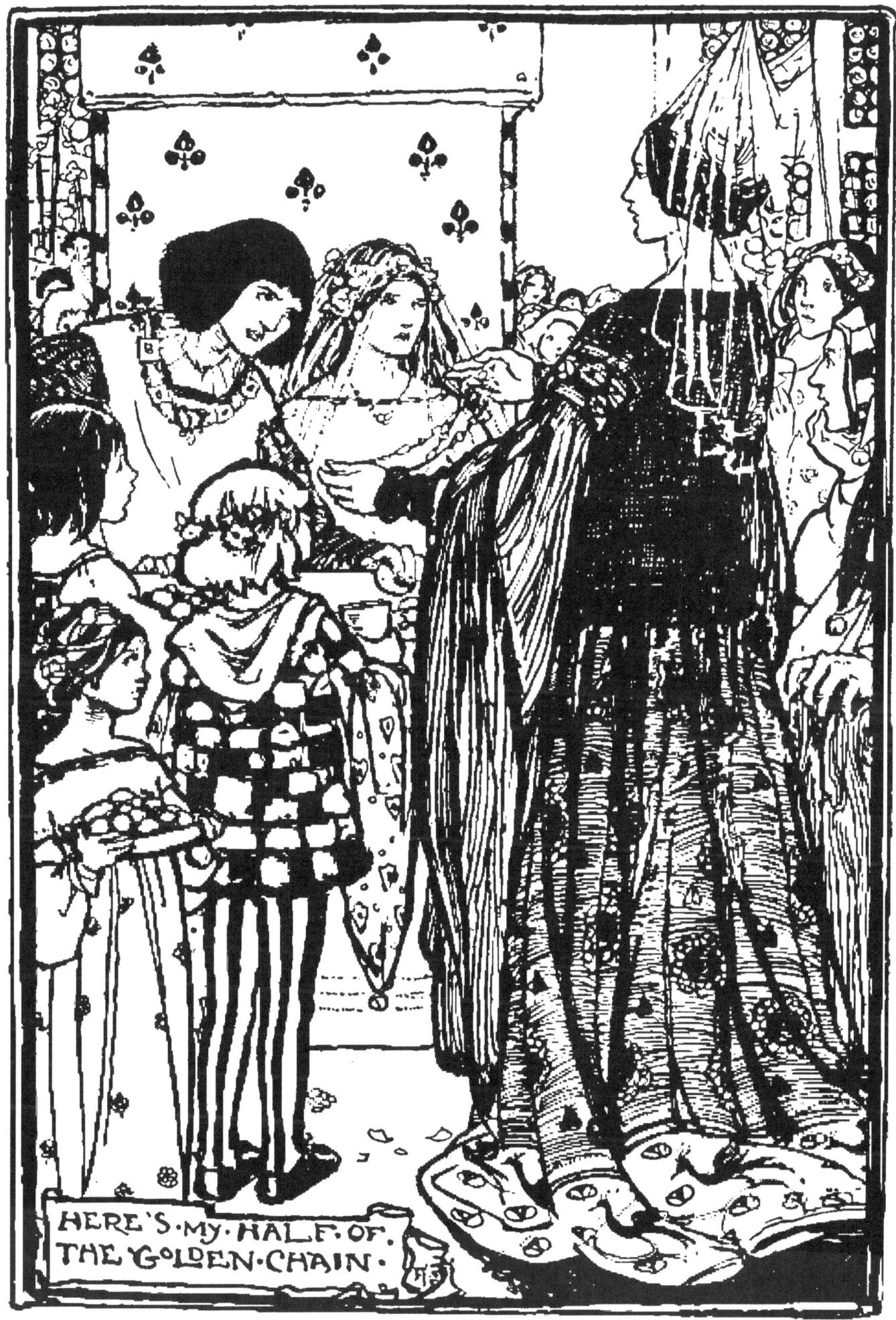

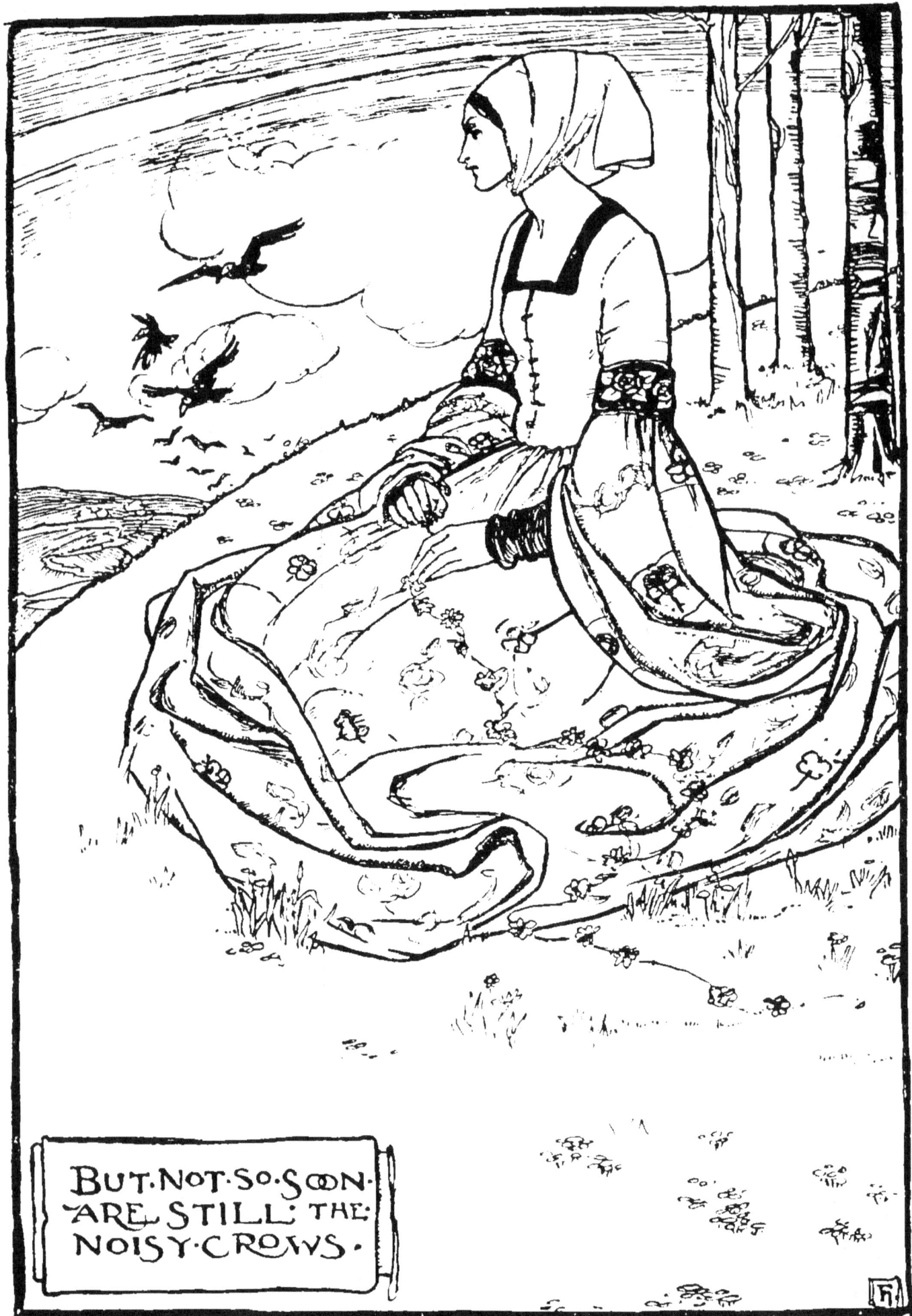

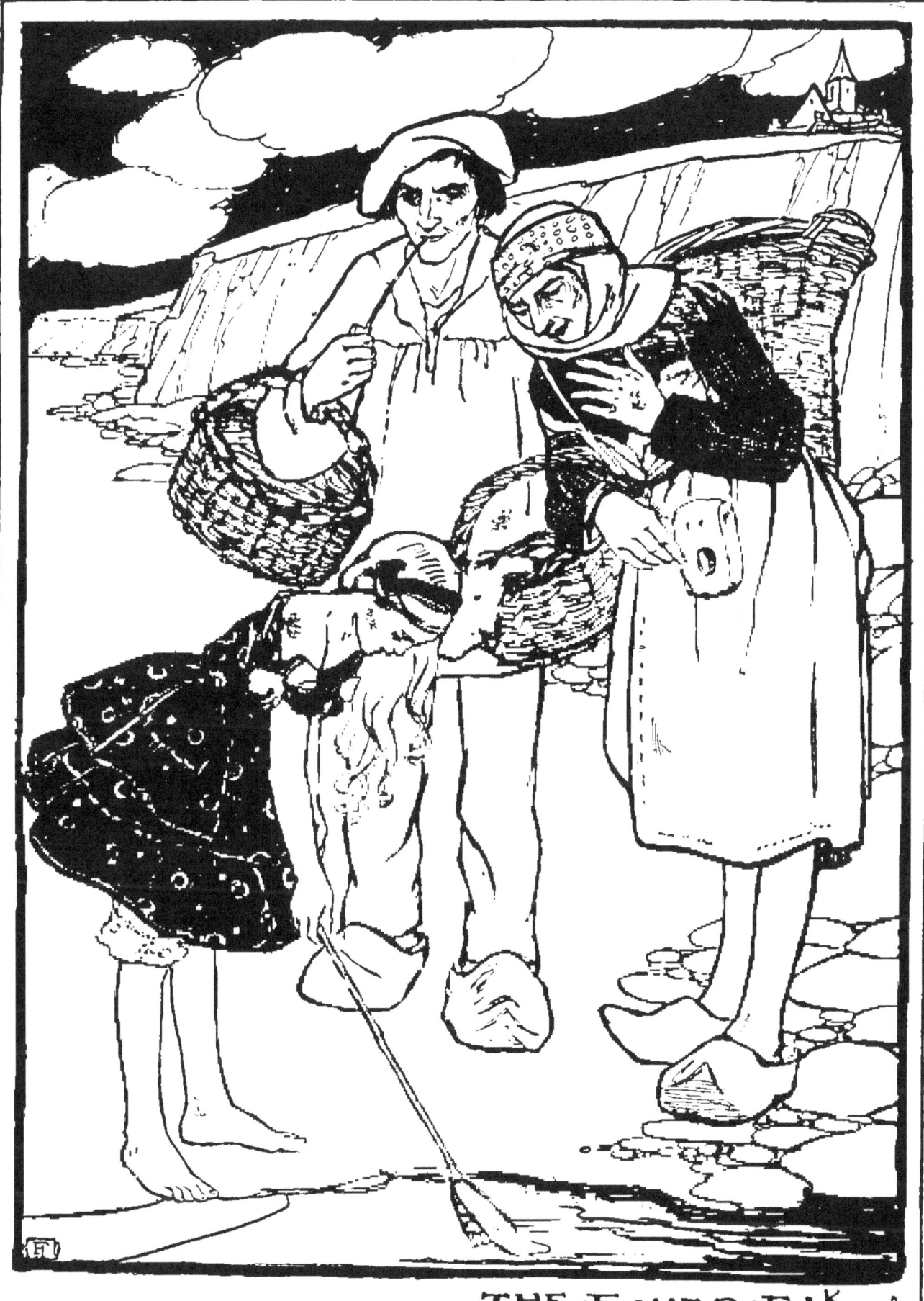

THE FISHER FOLK WOULD GIVE A KIND STRANGE WORD TO ME

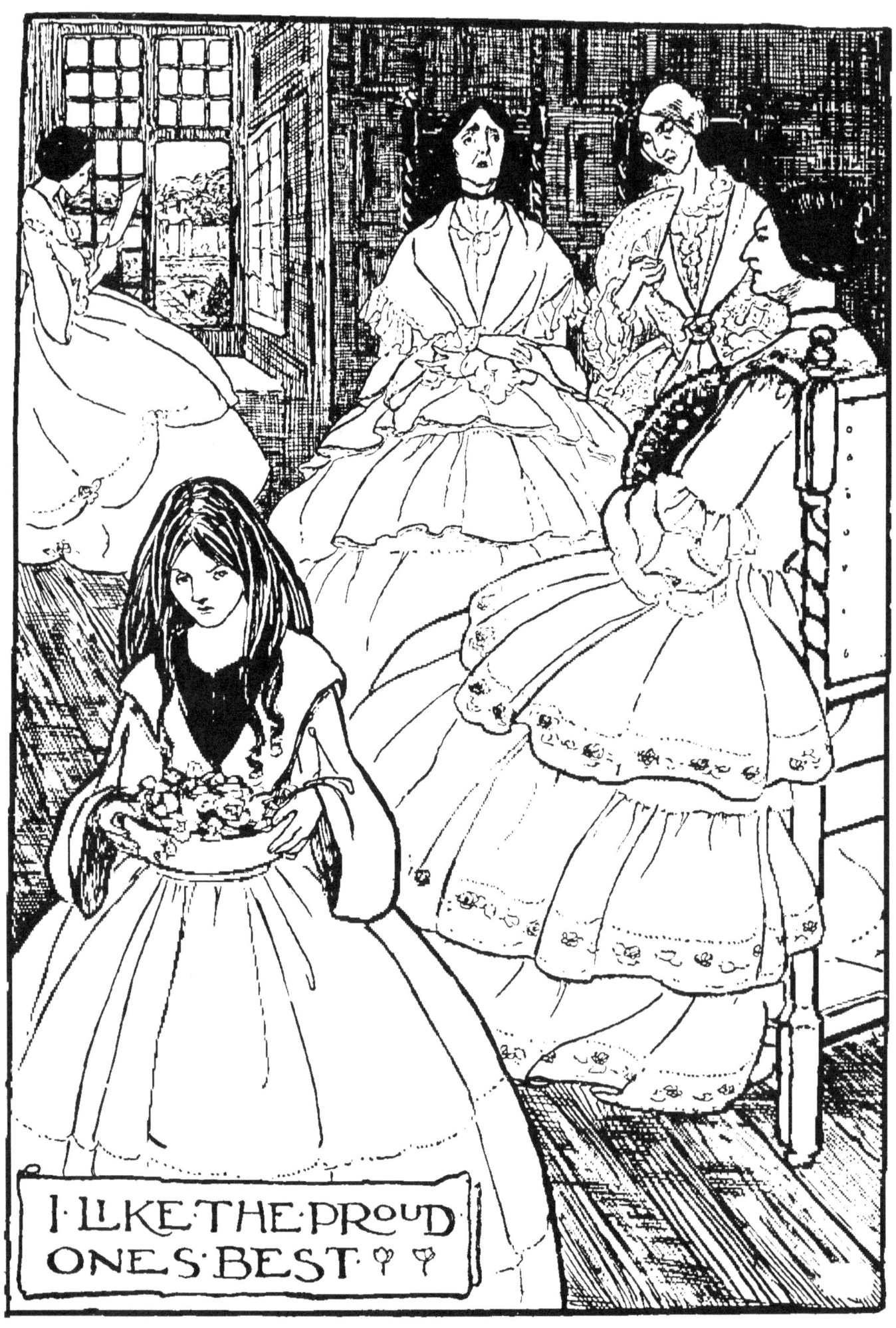

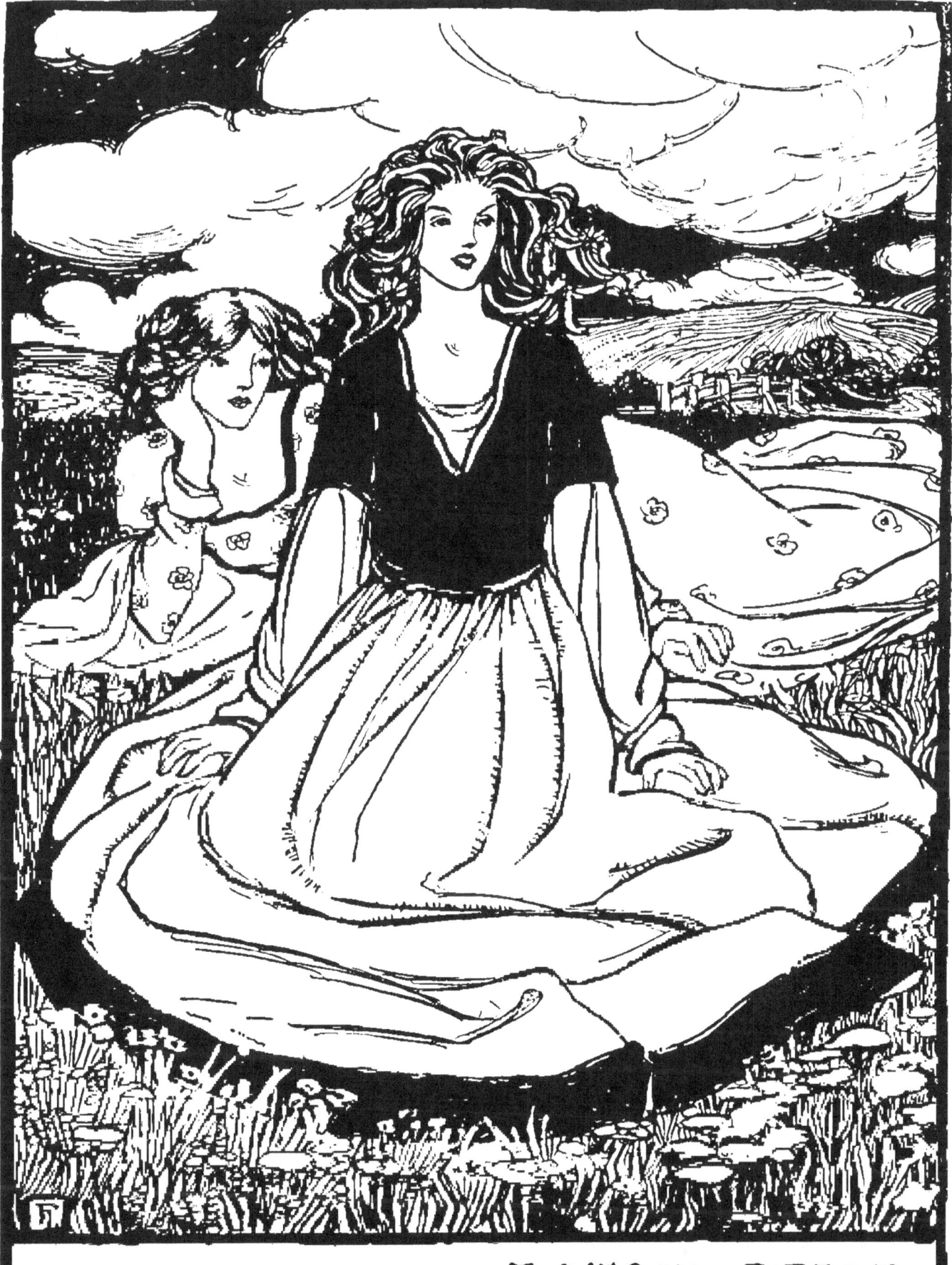

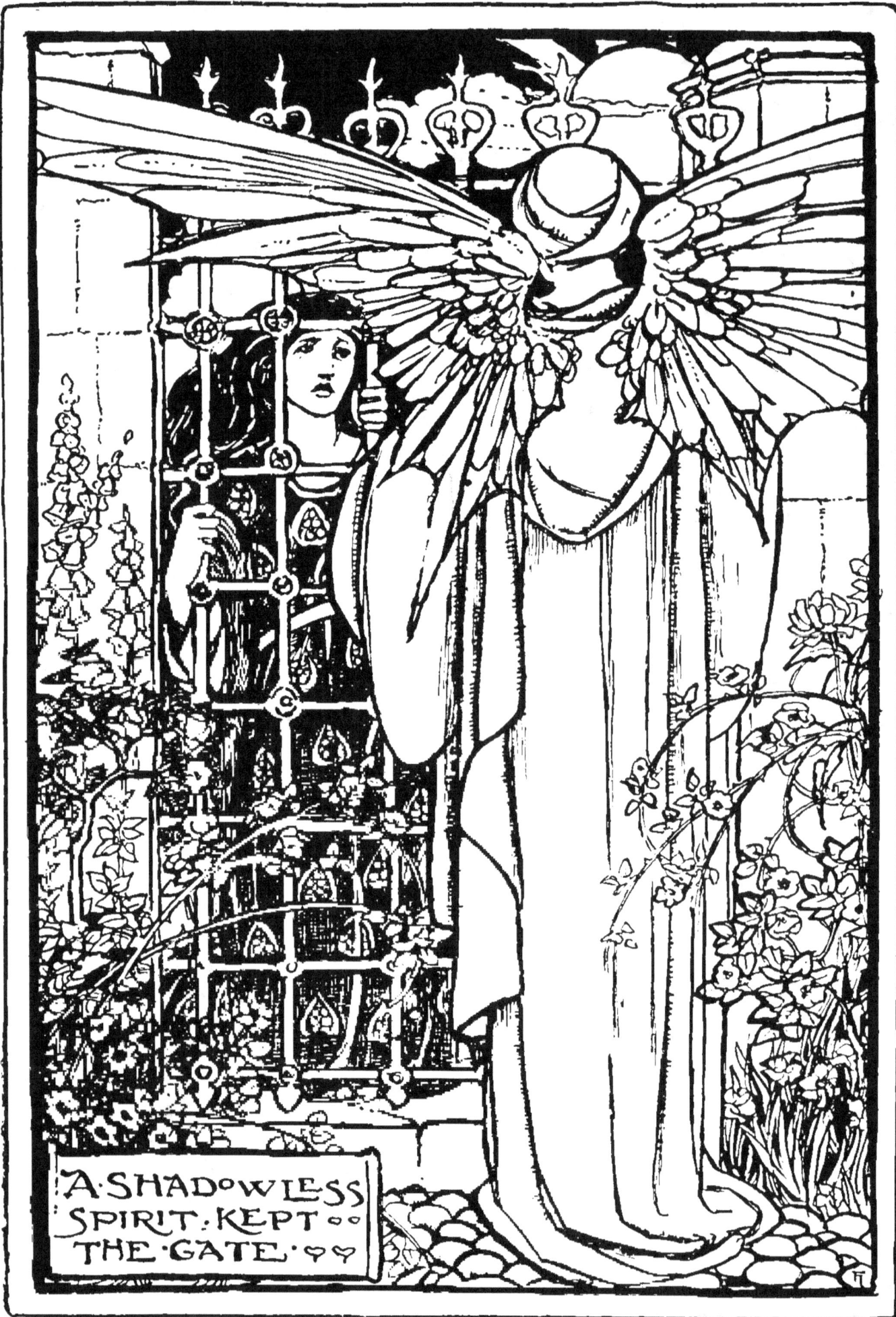

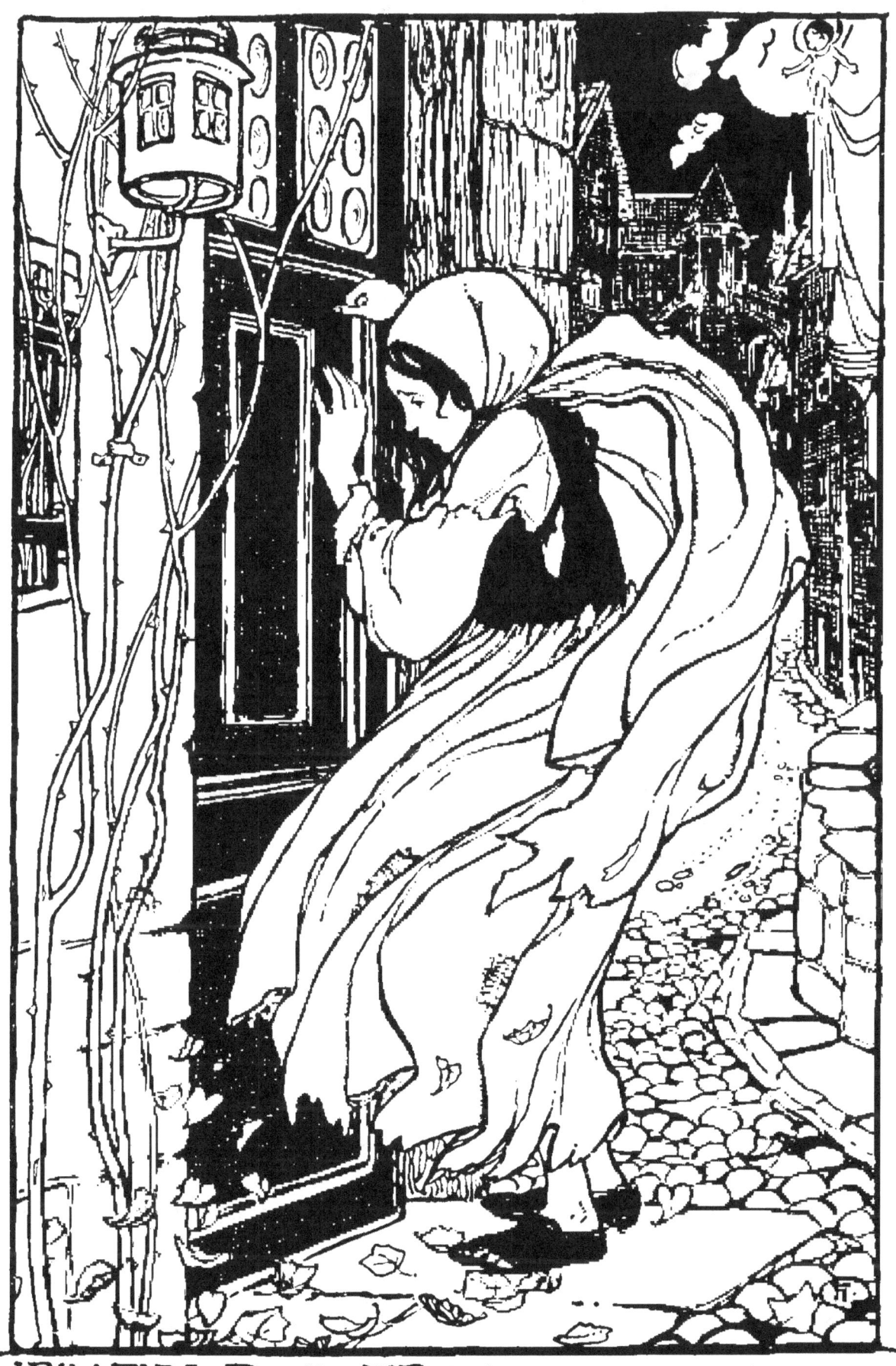

IF·IN·FIELD·OR·TREE·THERE·MIGHT·ONLY· BE·SUCH·A·WARM·SOFT·SLEEPING·PLACE· FOUND·FOR·ME·

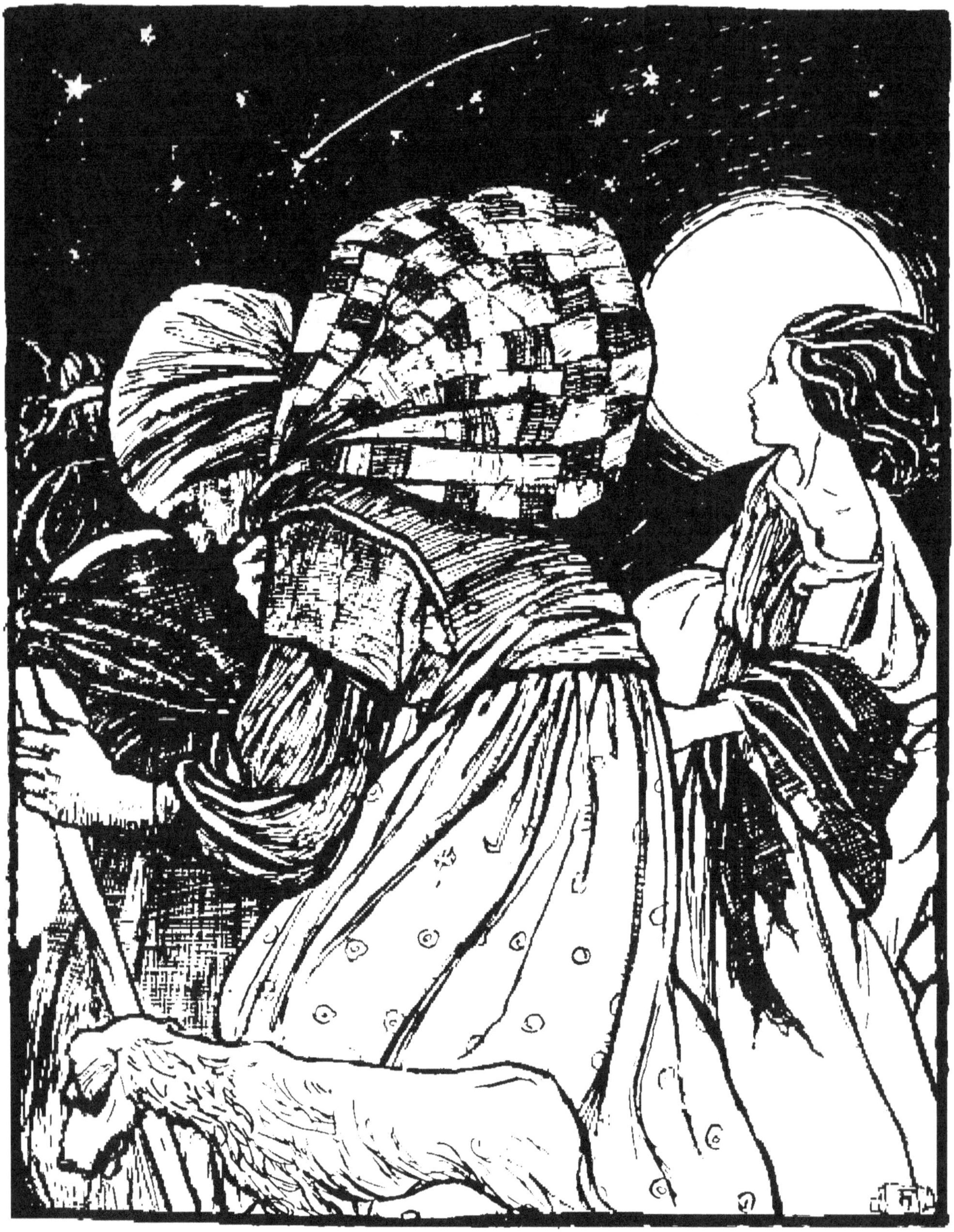

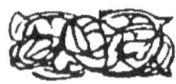 LIFE·IS·NOT·SWEET·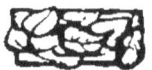

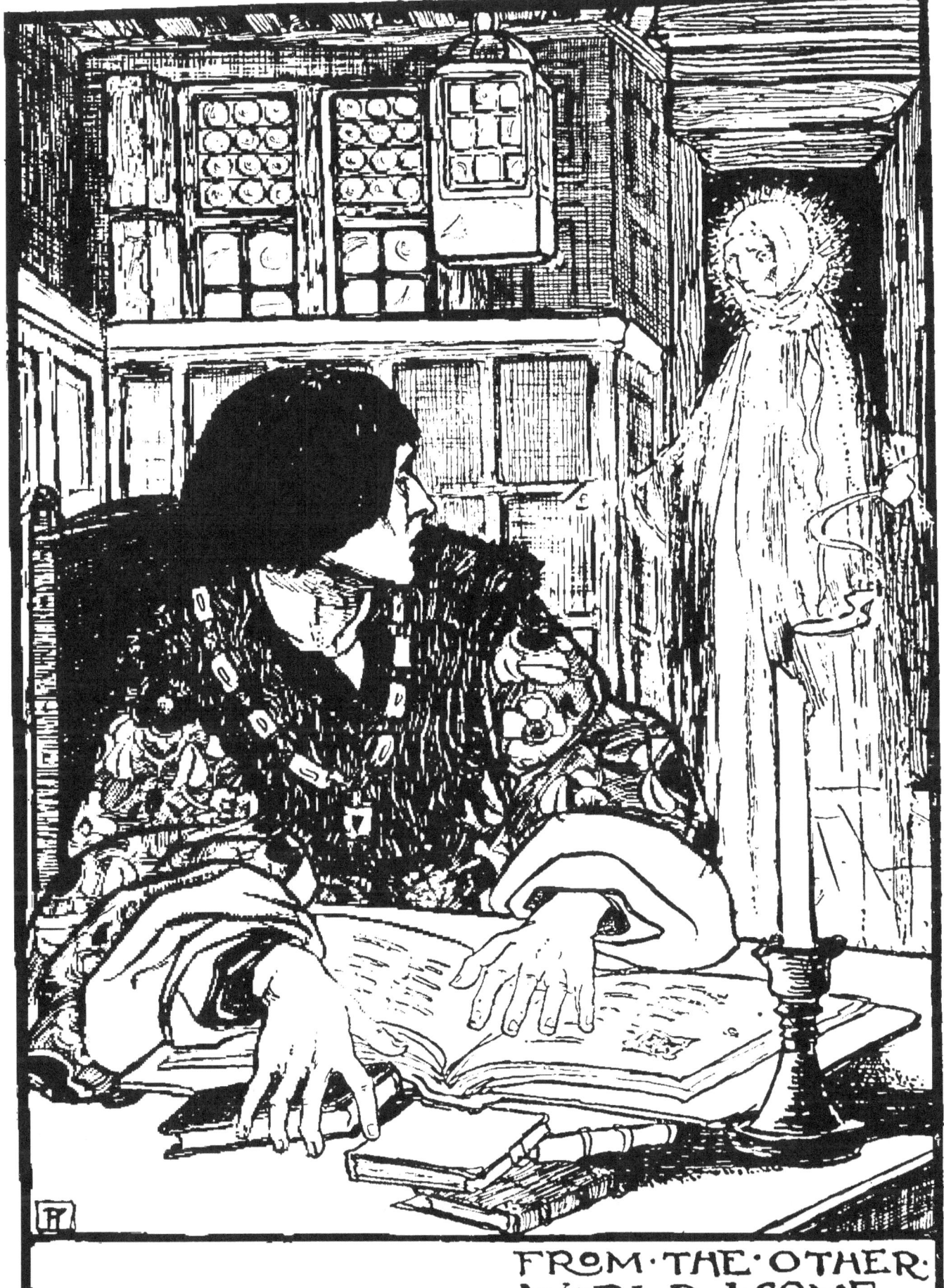

FROM·THE·OTHER·
WORLD·I·COME·
BACK·TO·YOU

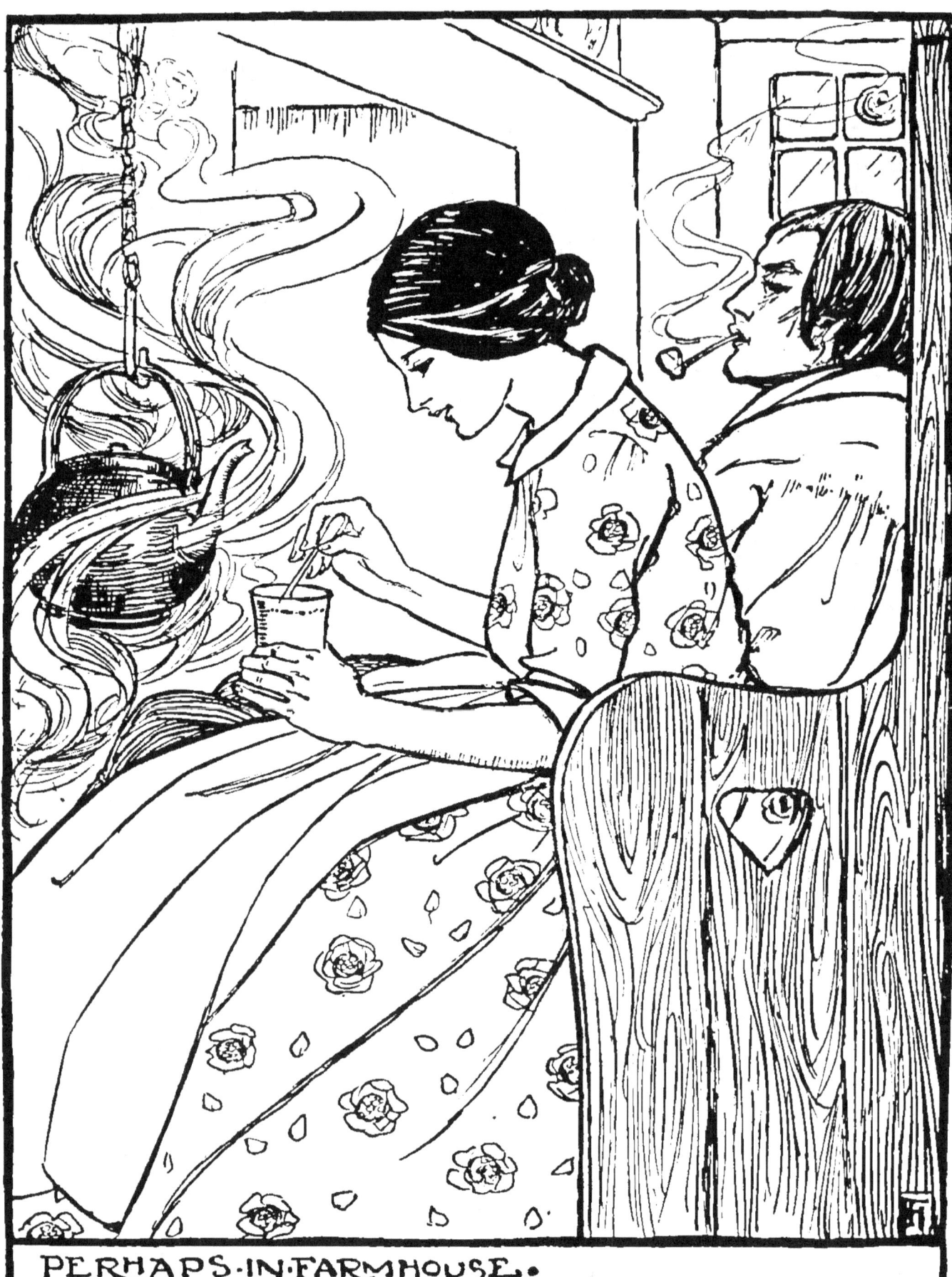

PERHAPS IN FARMHOUSE
OF HER OWN
SOME HUSBAND KEEPS
HER COSY.

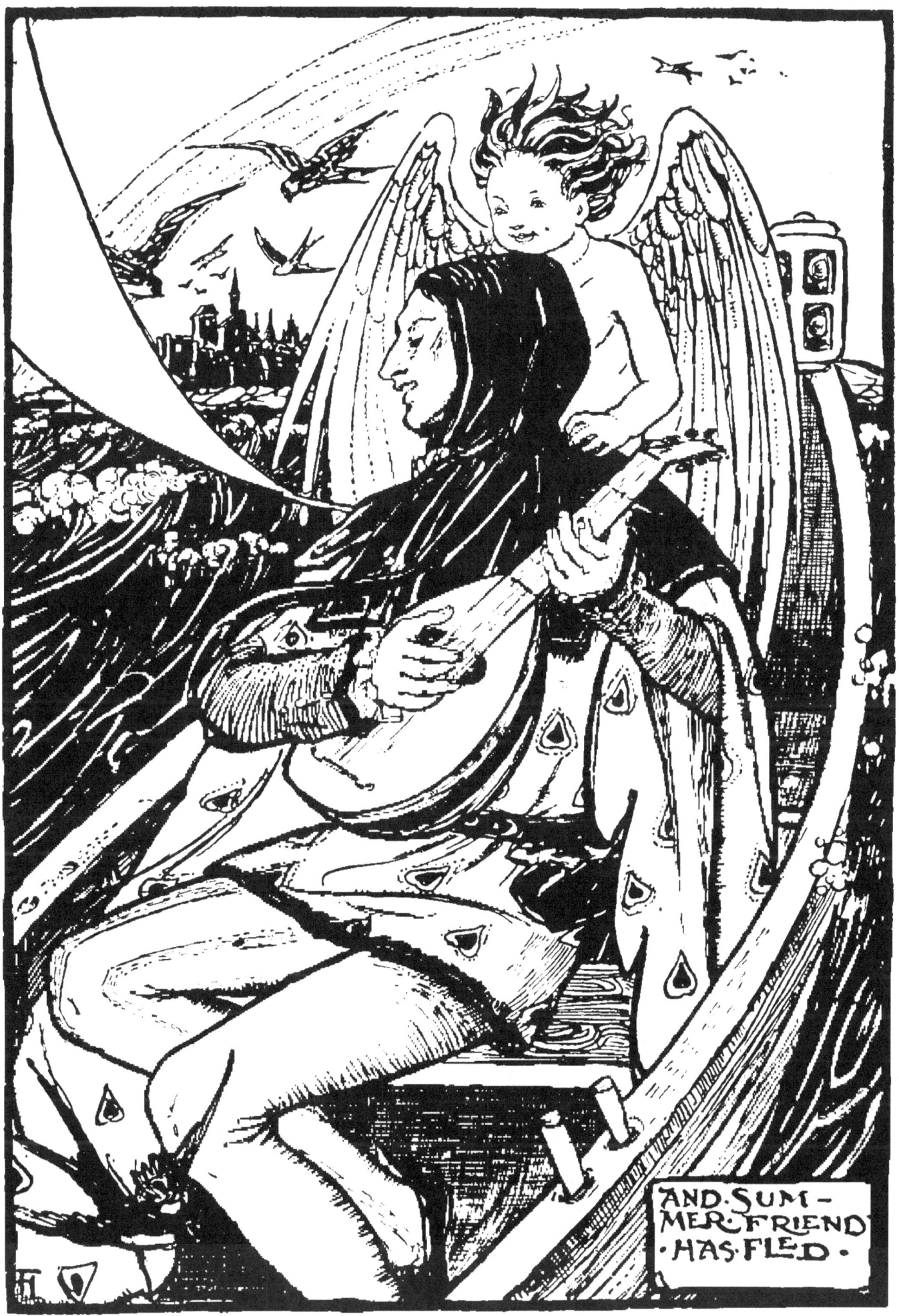

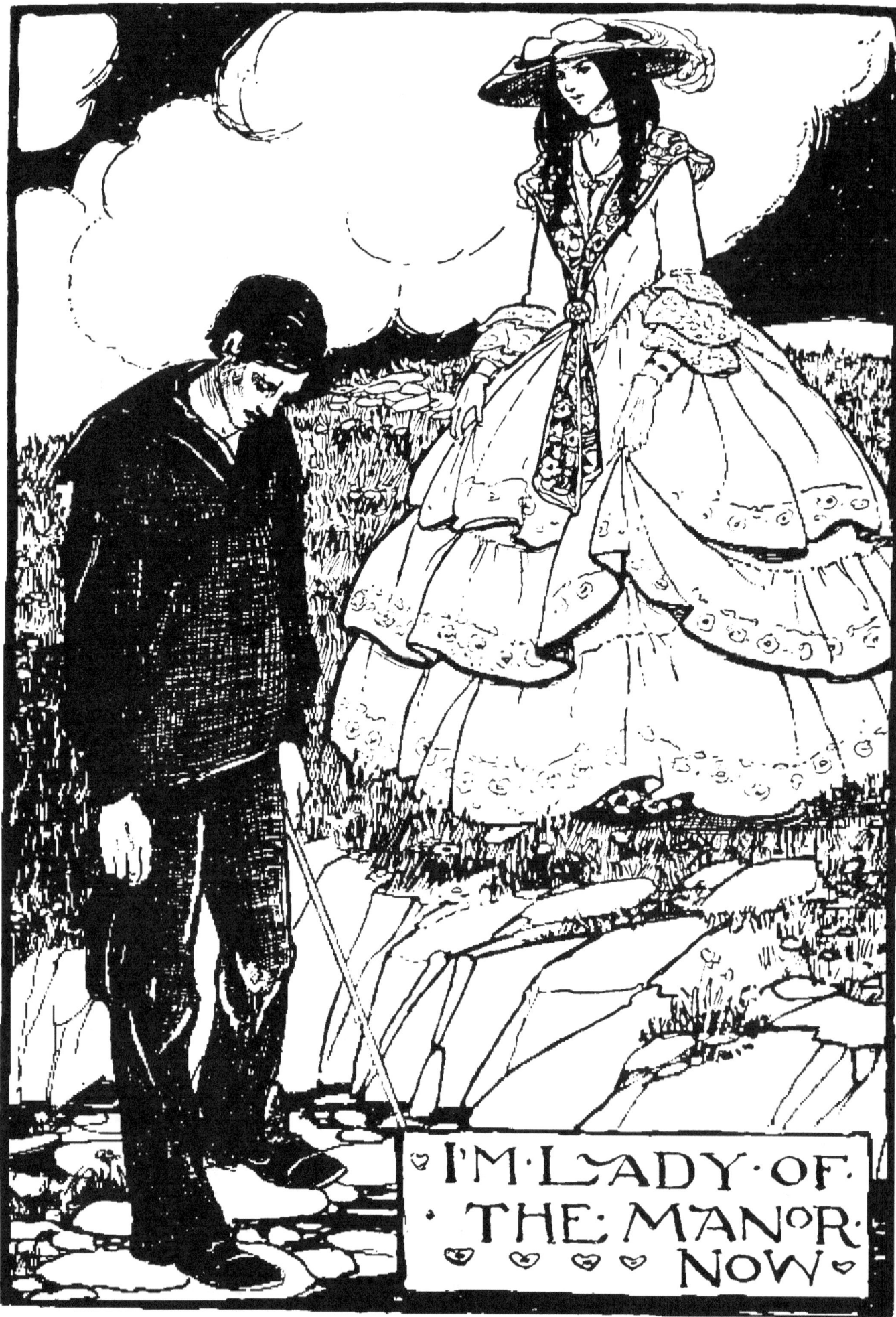

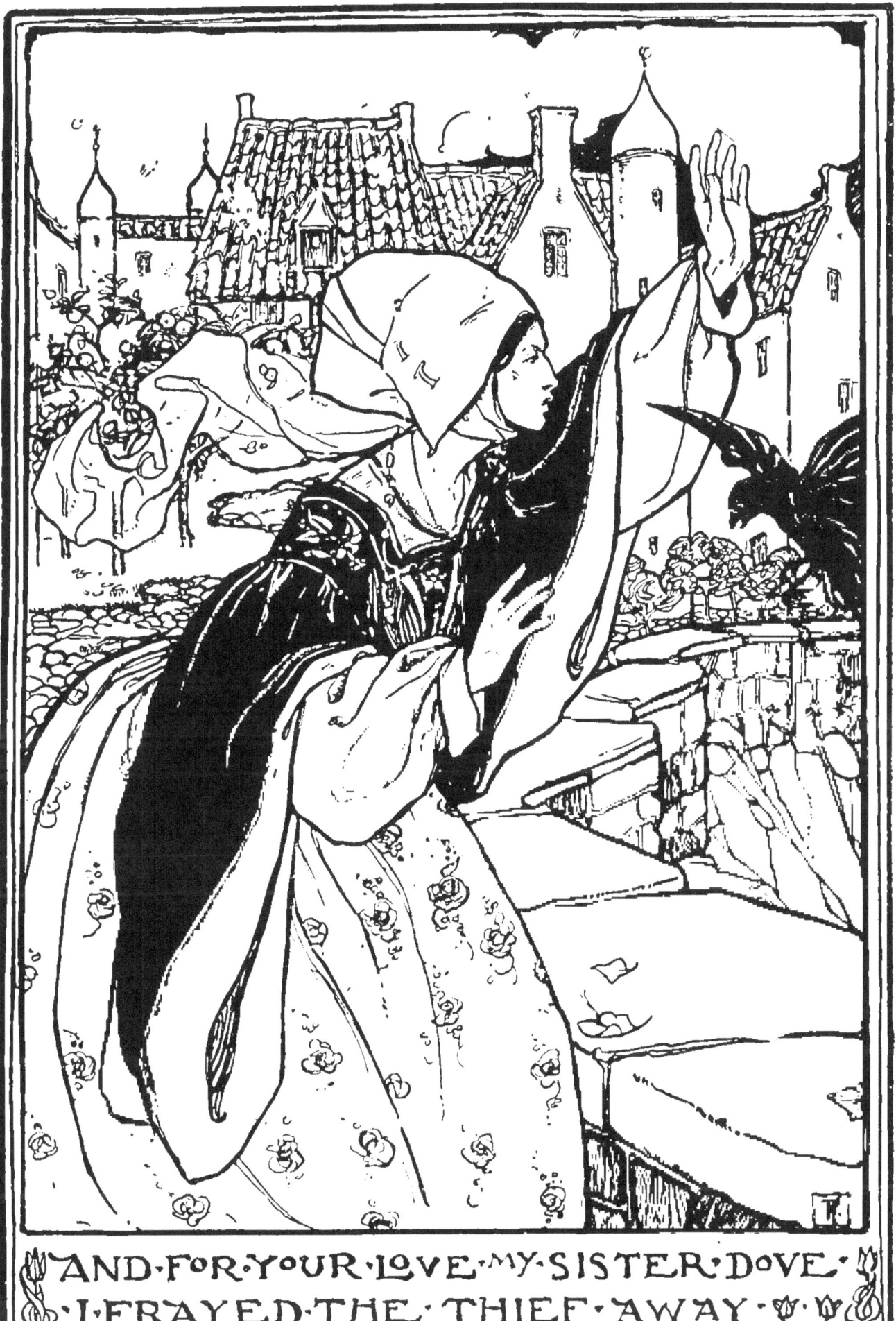

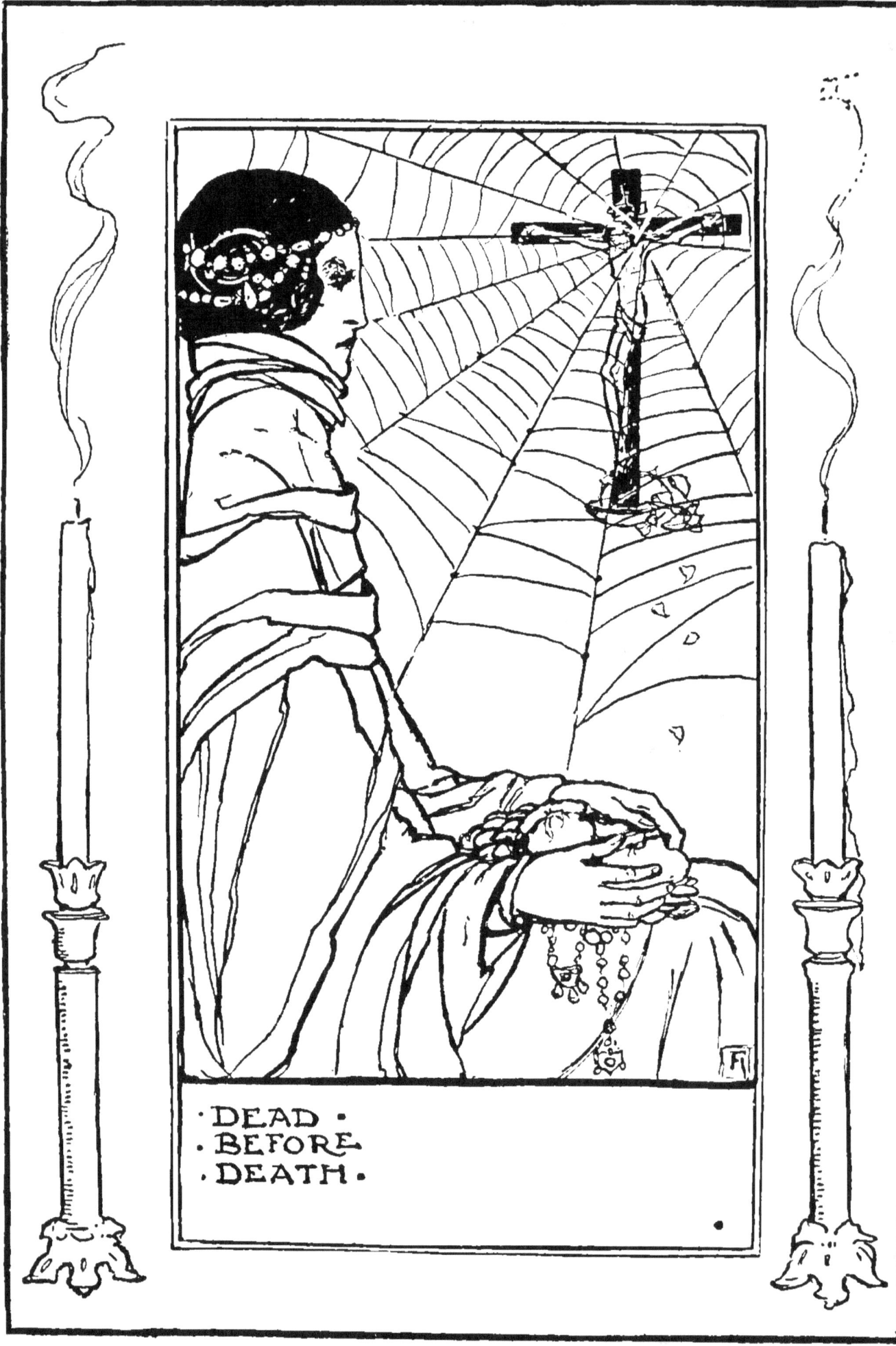

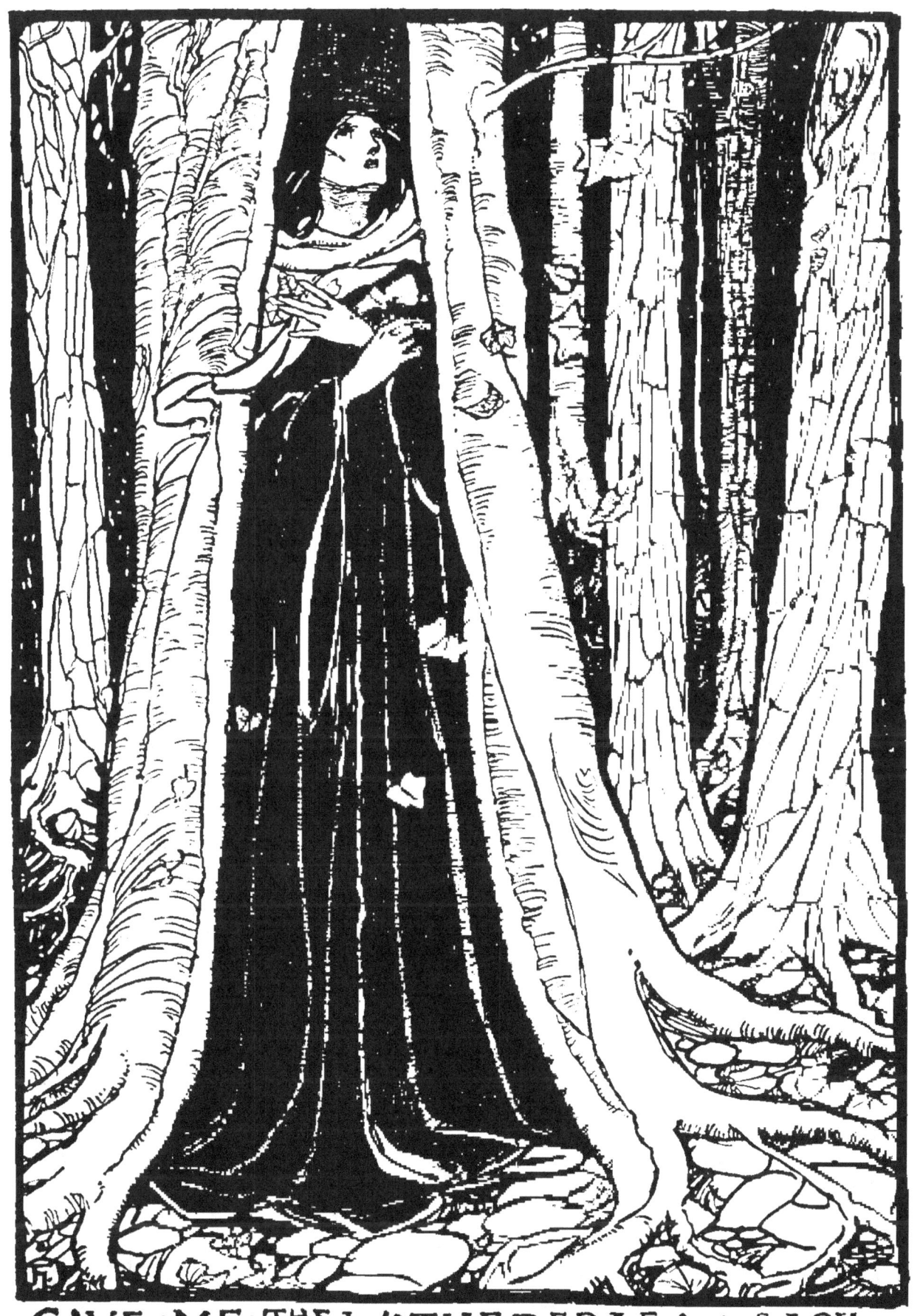

GIVE ME THE WITHERED LEAVES I CHOSE BEFORE IN THE OLD TIME

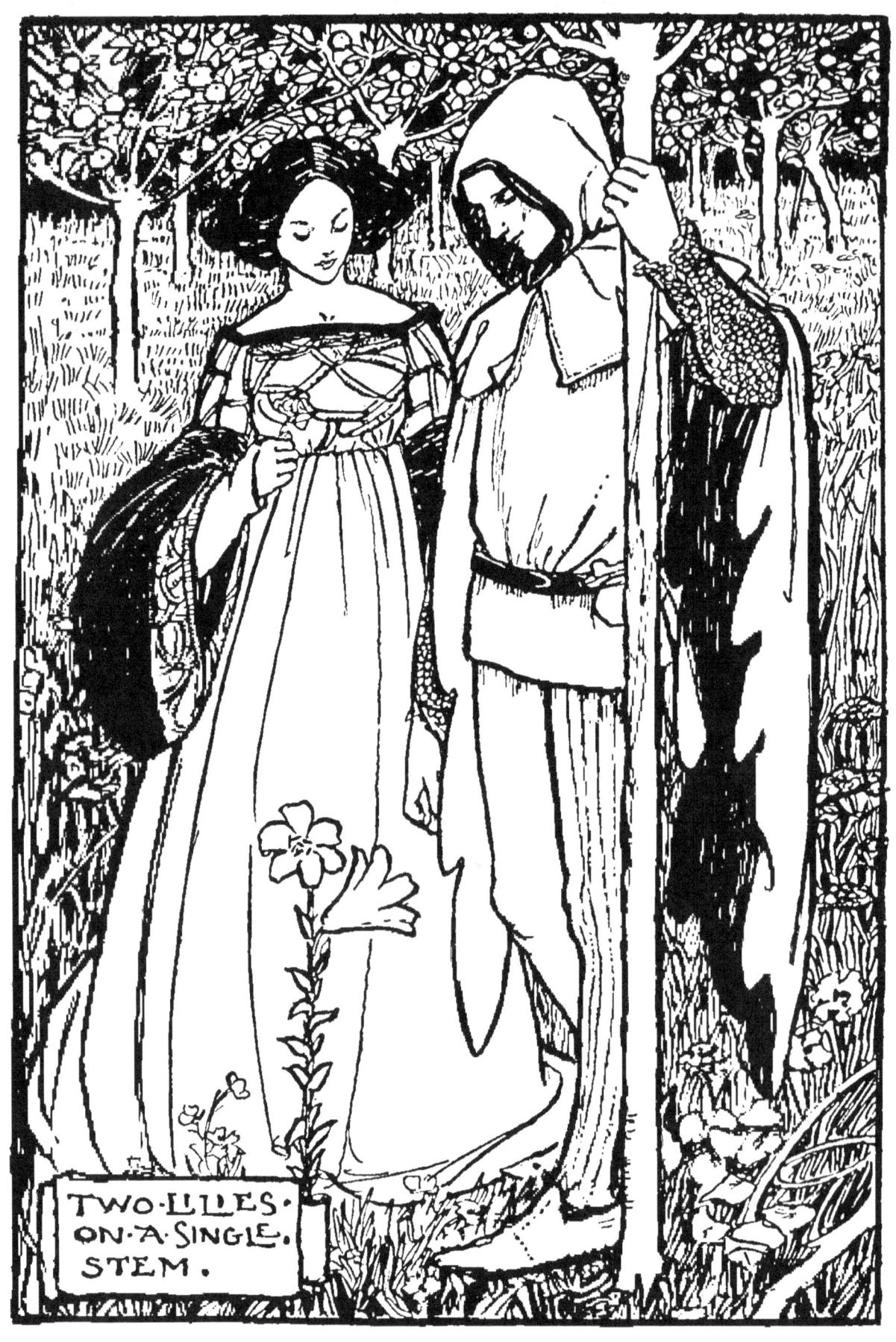

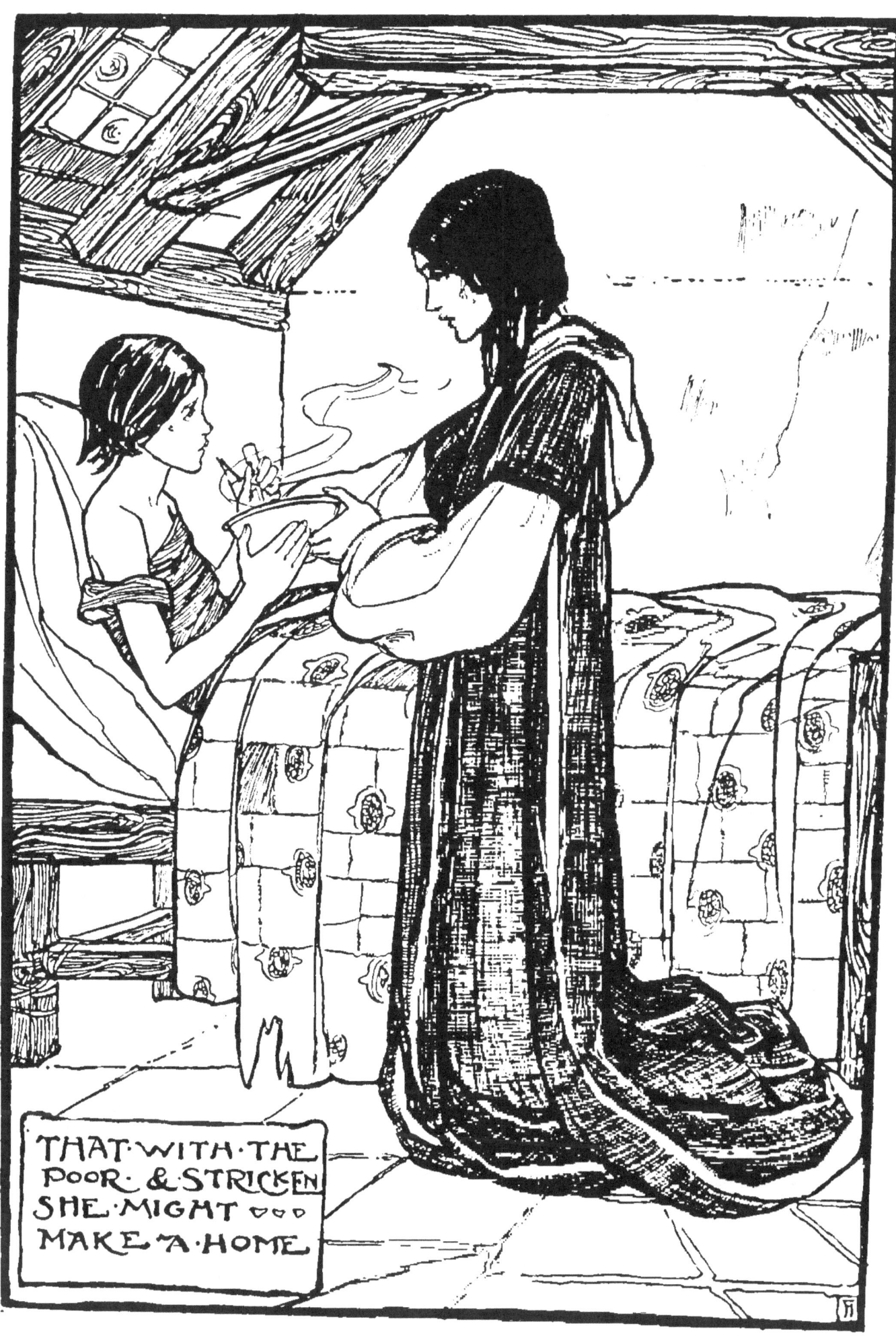

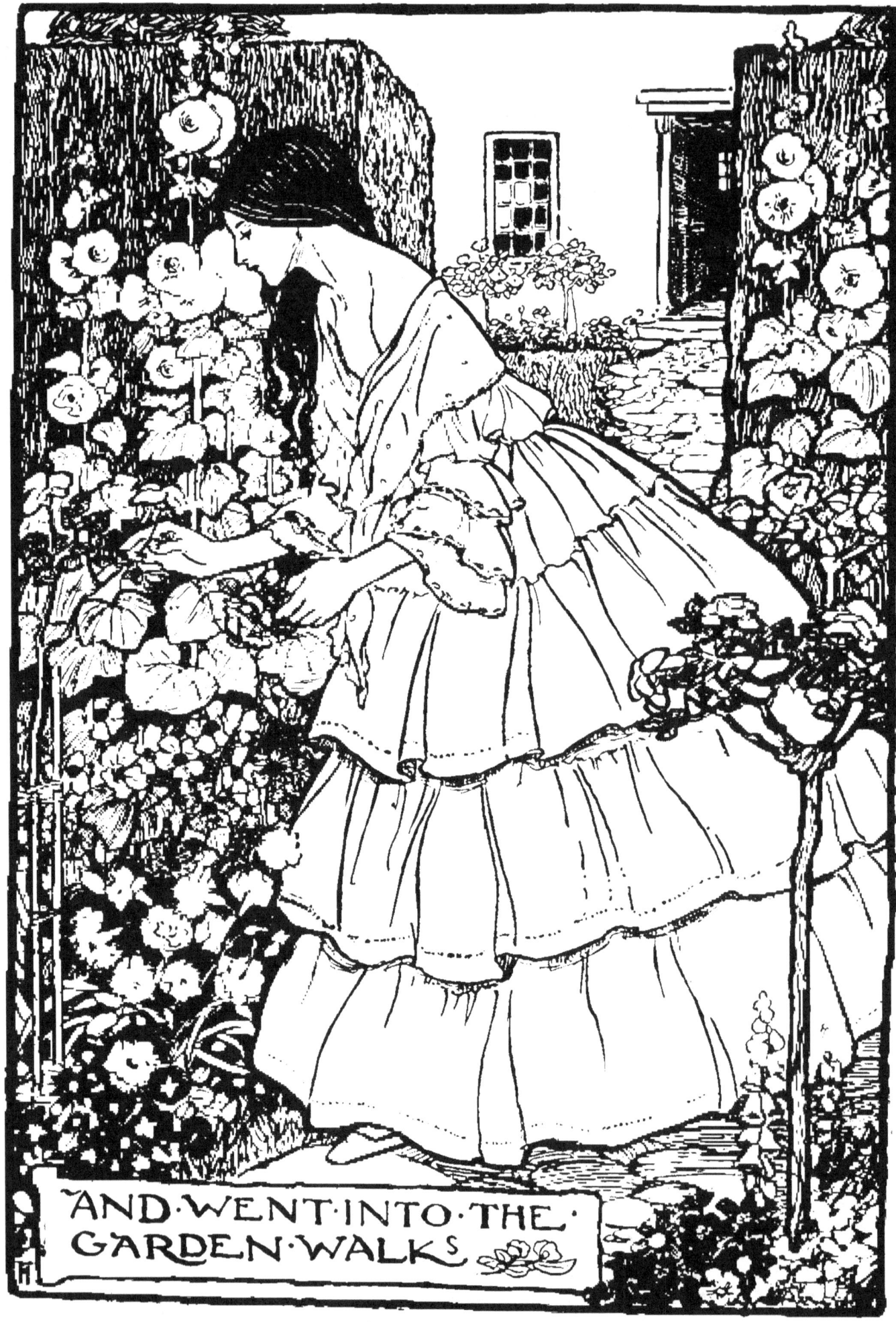

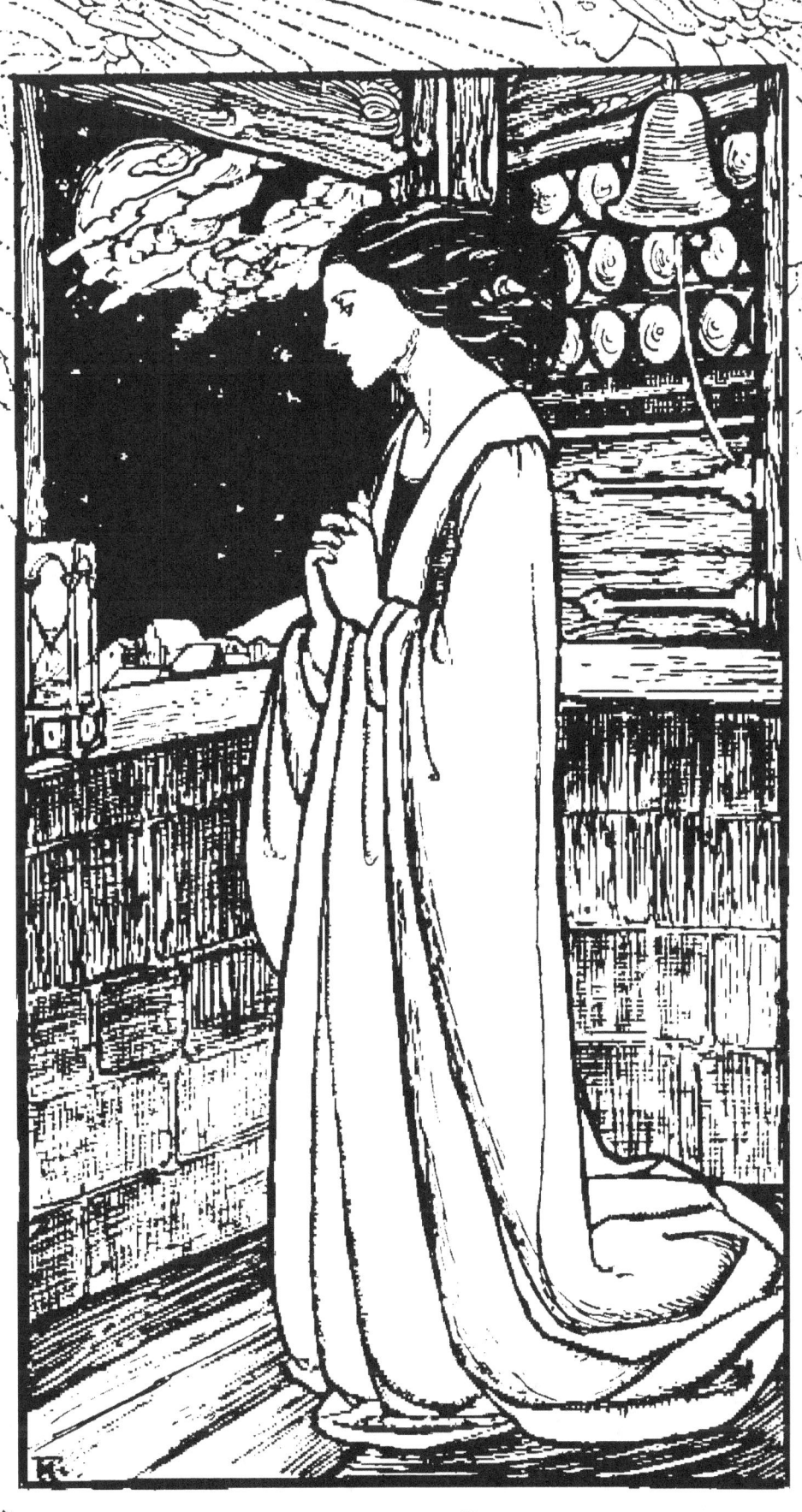

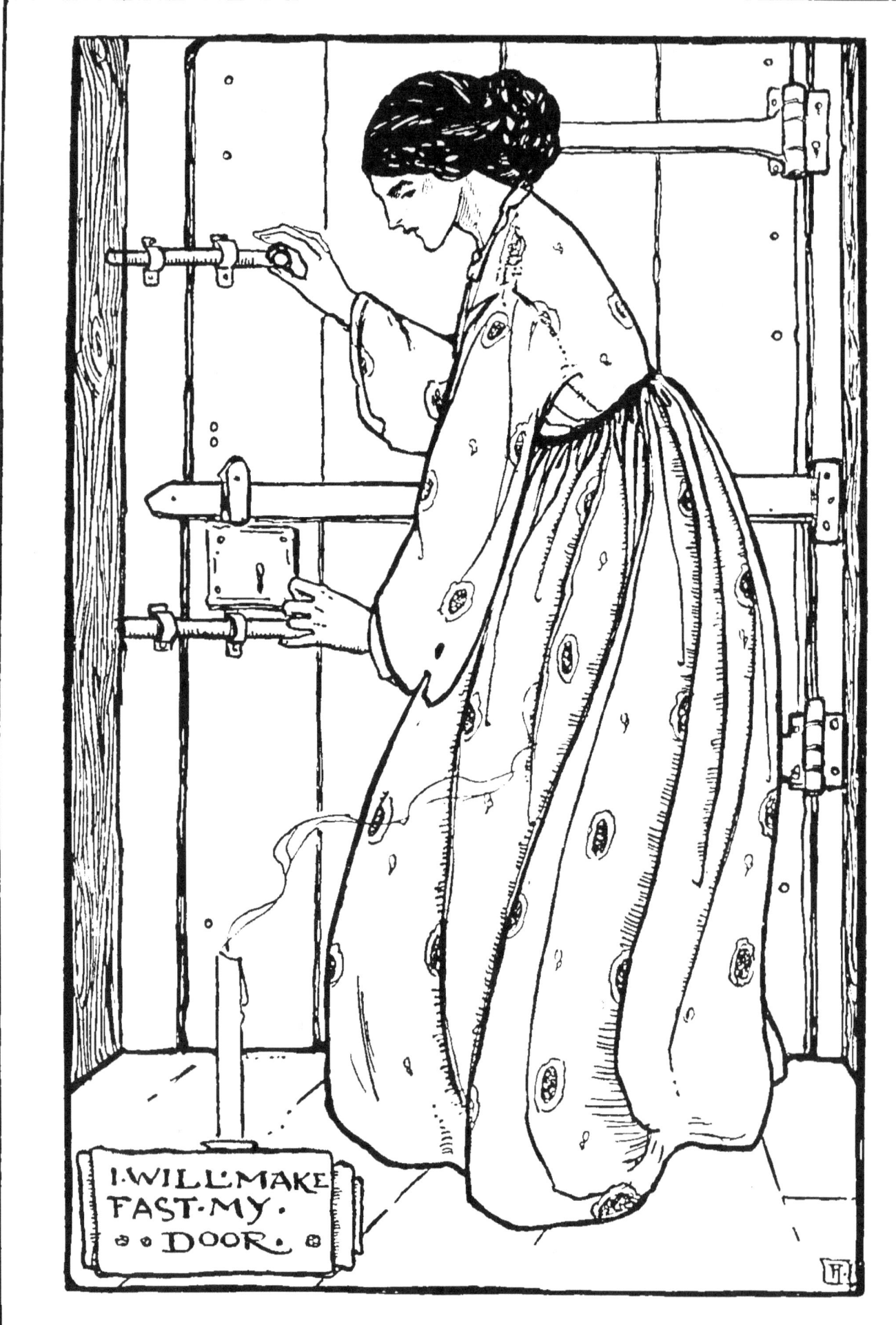

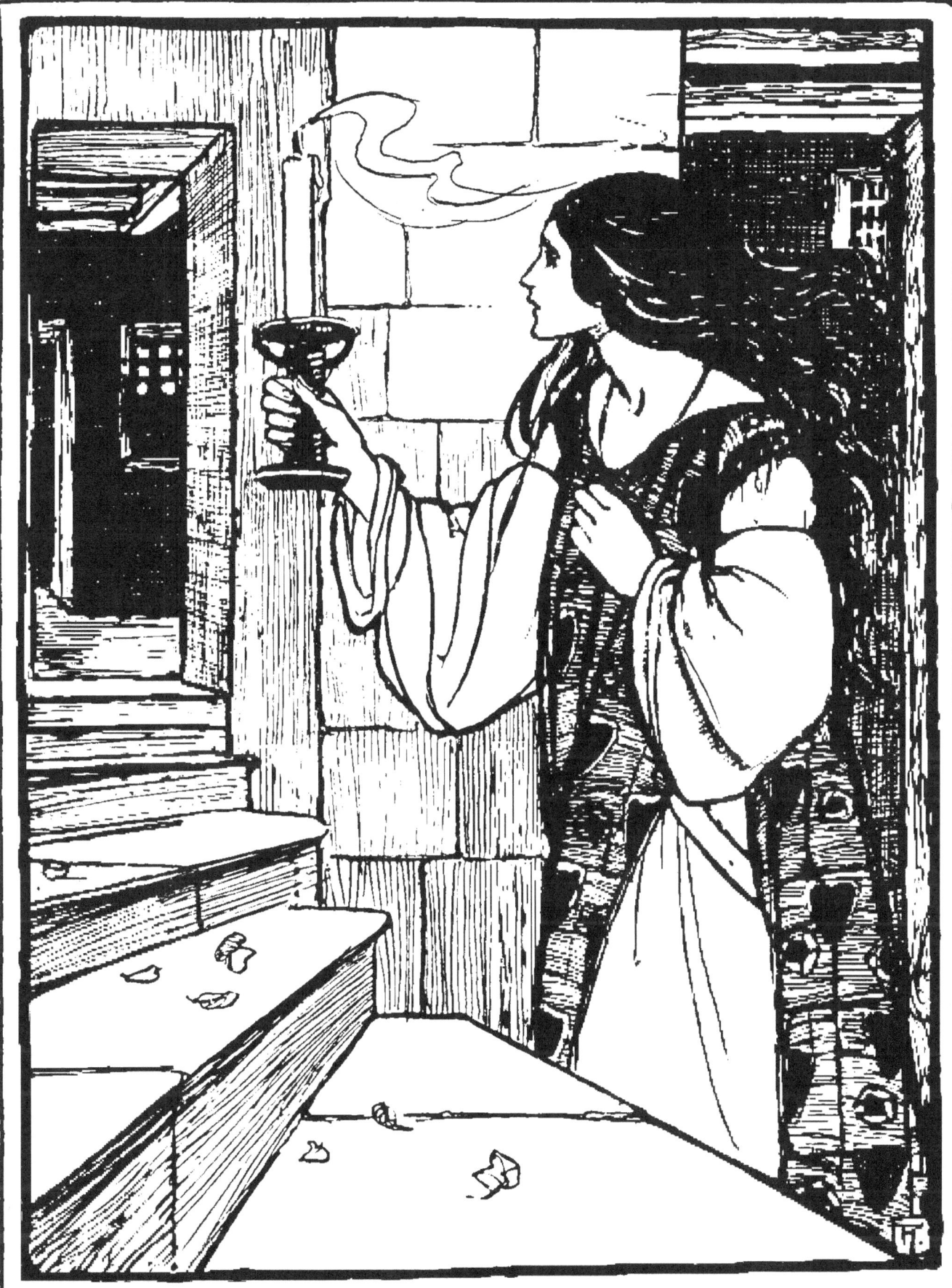

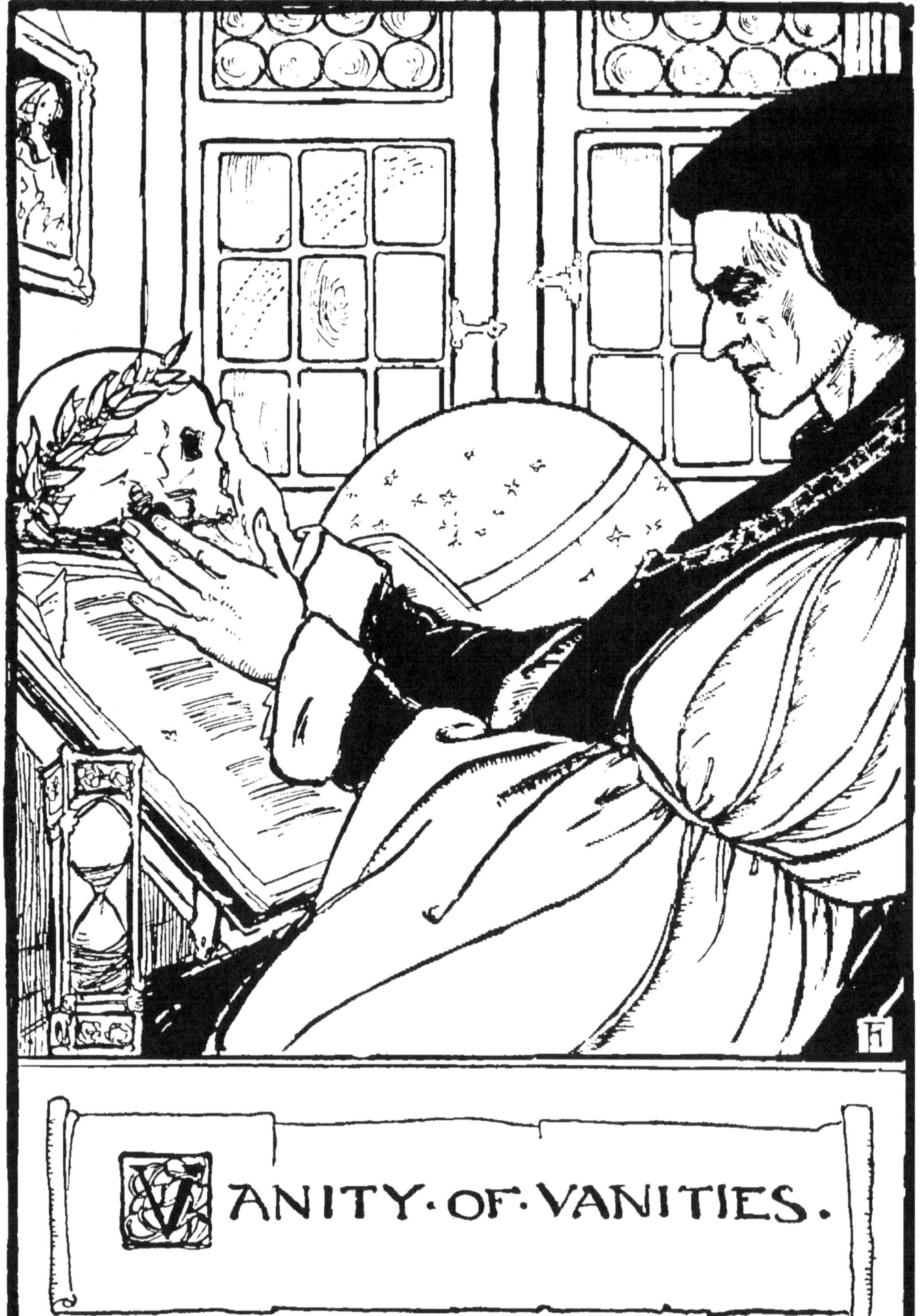

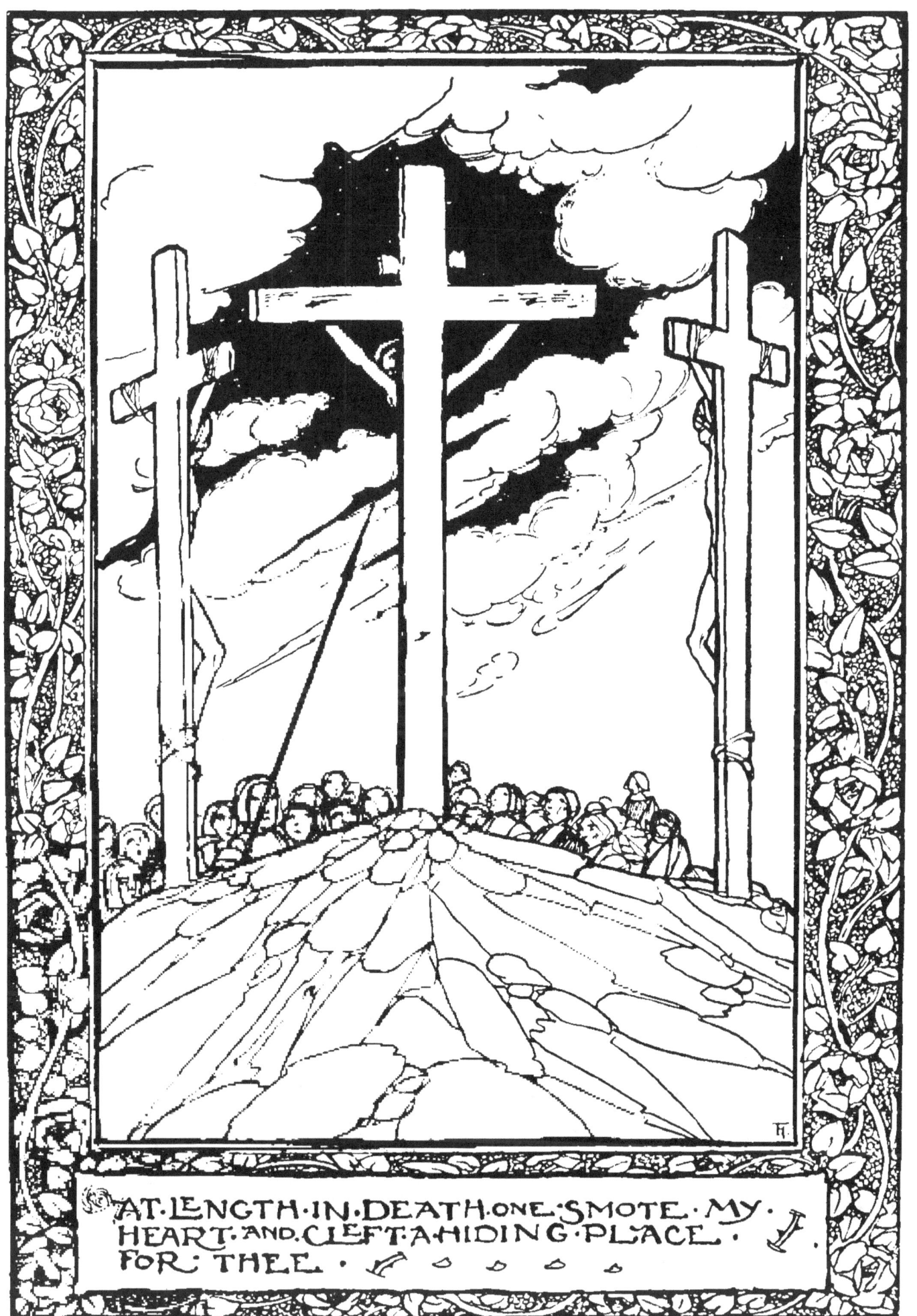

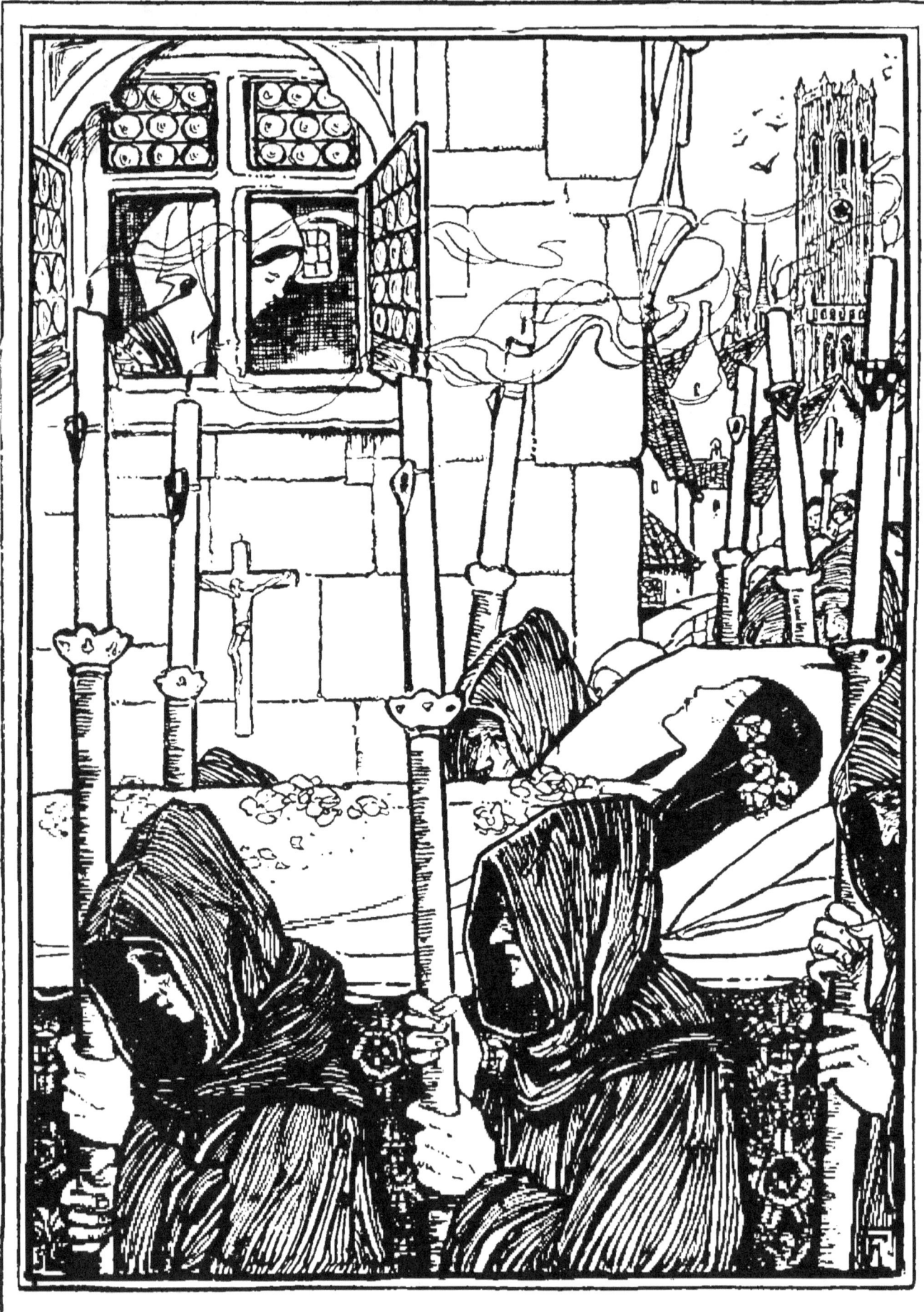

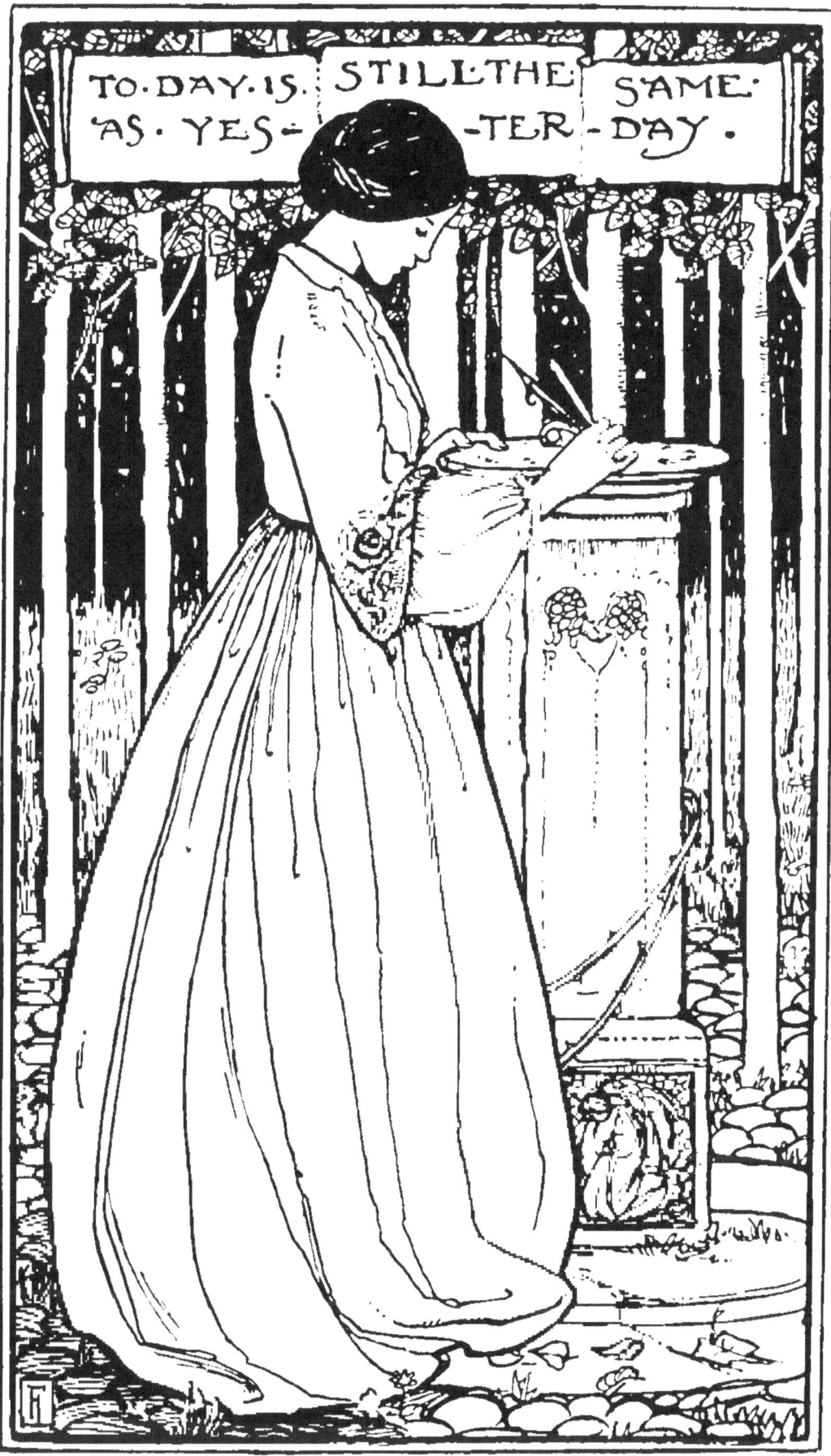

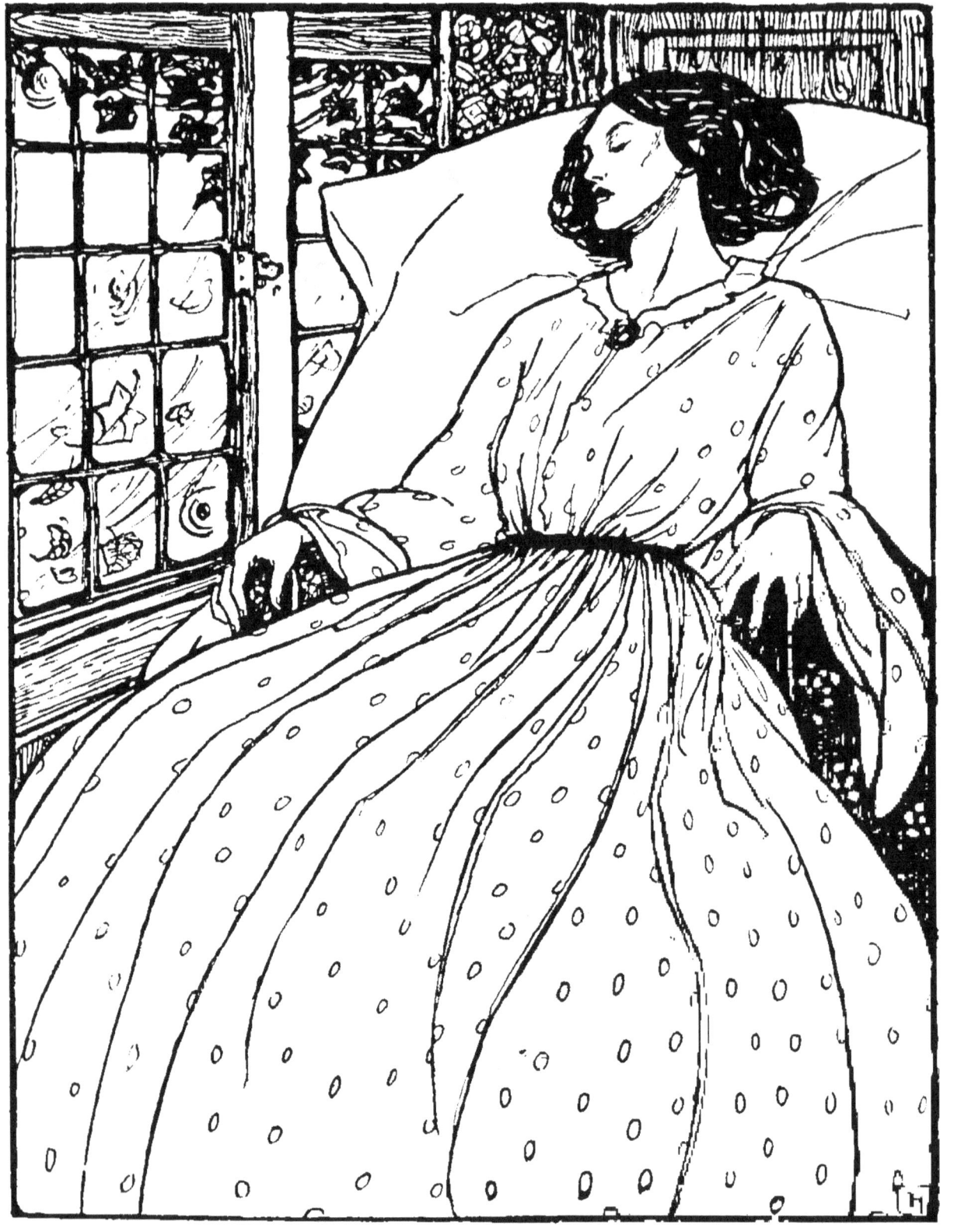

I·FORGET·HOW·SUMMER·
GLOWED·AND·SHONE·
WHILE·AUTUMN·GRIPS·
ME·WITH·ITS·FINGERS·
WAN·